WHAT IF MONEY GREW ON TREES?

WHAT IF MONEY GREW ON TREES?

Asking the big questions about economics

editor
DAVID BOYLE

foreword by
NEVA GOODWIN

METRO BOOKS
New York

METRO BOOK
New York

An Imprint of Sterling Publishing
1166 Avenue of the Americas
New York, NY 10036

© 2013 by Ivy Press Limited

This book was conceived, designed
and produced by **Ivy Press**
210 High Street
Lewes
East Sussex BN7 2NS
www.ivypress.co.uk

Creative Director: Peter Bridgewater
Publisher: Jason Hook
Art Director: Michael Whitehead
Editorial Director: Caroline Earle
Design: JC Lanaway
Illustrator: Ivan Hissey
Historical text and introductions: David Boyle

ISBN-13: 978-1-4351-5797-2

For information about custom editions,
special sales, and premium and corporate
purchases, please contact Sterling Special
Sales at 800-805-5489 or specialsales@
sterlingpublishing.com.

Manufactured in China
Color origination by Ivy Press Reprographics

2 4 6 8 10 9 7 5 3 1

www.sterlingpublishing.com

Contents

FOREWORD

More than four decades ago I was a young mother with very young children. I had never taken an economics course in school or college, but I had a burning question that caused me to seek out the Boston location of the US Statistical Office and pick up a copy of the statistical abstract of the US Census, 1970. I was intensely conscious of the economic value of parenting, home health, and nutrition activities, and other kinds of homemaking, and painfully aware of how little society tends to value that work or pay for it. I wondered how much we would have to tax paid work to pay for the absolutely vital caring work. (After many hours poring over my statistical abstract I came to the conclusion it was at least 25 percent.)

What made me feel as well as think was looking at the statistics for agriculture—seeing the number of farms in the USA decreasing year after year. I remember sitting with tears running down my face, because I knew how much heartache went with the loss of those farms. Irish playwright (and cofounder of the London School of Economics) George Bernard Shaw used to say that it took "a civilized man" to be "deeply moved by statistics." That may be so, but it convinced me—as a relatively civilized woman—that it also took an economist. So, realizing that I was heading inevitably for a career change, I went back to college and became one.

To start with, the question I most wanted to answer was "Why don't our wages reflect the real value of work to society?" I have also been motivated by a range of related questions, such as "How might the economic system reflect our human values better than it does at the moment?"

Since then, I have been a working economist, and have written textbooks and struggled to fill in some of the gaps in our understanding about the things that really matter. The heart of economics needs to be asking difficult questions about the world. This is a book of difficult questions, too, asking "What if?" sometimes about the present and sometimes about what actually happened in history. The answers are not definitive—they are written by a range of people who do not necessarily agree with one another. But they are designed to encourage people to think deeply about the way the world is, and the way the economic system is—and whether it might be different.

The questions cover everything from money to work and beyond, and I hope that reading the book will get people into the habit of asking difficult questions themselves. Why do we believe in money? What choices—or lack of choices—lead us to the work that fills our lives? Why do bankers get paid so much more than nurses? Because the questions we ask are not just the beginning of wisdom, they are also the beginning of change. To quote George Bernard Shaw again: 'some men see things as they are and ask why; others dream things that never were and ask why not." I might also add: they ask "What if?"

Neva Goodwin
Codirector of the Global Development and Environment Institute at
Tufts University, near Boston, Massachusetts, and lead author
of *Microeconomics in Context* and *Macroeconomics in Context*.

INTRODUCTION

Economics began with the ancient Greeks, and came into its own after the Scottish moral philosopher Adam Smith published his book *The Wealth of Nations* in 1776. The next generation or two threw up a whole range of statisticians, political economists, and mathematicians who founded the discipline we know today.

But it is a strange discipline, part art, part science—with advocates on both sides. Some economists prefer graphs and formulae; some prefer—as the great British economist John Maynard Keynes put it—an idea that starts with "a great woolly monster inside my head." These days, the emphasis is on the graphs, so much so that in 1999 there was an uprising against economics teaching at La Sorbonne in Paris by students who wanted to be taught in what they called a less "autistic" manner.

The Post-Autistic Economics movement begun by these students had an important objective, which was to make sure that all those formulae and models of the way that money works did not prevent economists from being able to see the real world. They wanted economists to understand the insights that other disciplines, like psychology or biology, can provide about the way people live, behave, and spend their money.

The Sorbonne students achieved their objective. There was a government inquiry into economics teaching which vindicated them, and the curriculum was changed. There were also follow-up petitions along similar lines by economics graduates in other parts of the world. However, despite this success, there is still an issue about the way some mainstream economics departments cling to their formulae, allowing them to compromise with the way the real world actually works—and forget that economic history was once full of other possibilities.

So let us dream for a moment that economics was not, as they say, the "dismal science," and was really the barefoot, enthusiastic business that its greatest proponents would like it to be. Let us imagine that you could be an amateur economist, armed only with a notebook and a calculator, going out like Sherlock Holmes to understand a complex world. Because that is what we have tried to achieve in this book.

We have asked a number of economists and economics writers, who come from very different points of view, to do what economists are trained to do, which is to predict and to explain. What would happen if money grew on trees? What would happen if a whole number of shifts occurred in the way that the economy or the world happens to work at the moment? Don't let us guess the answers—let us have expert speculations by people who have been wondering about these issues for their whole lives.

So that is what *What if Money Grew on Trees?* tries to do. It suggests what the implications and causalities would be if the world changed and, by doing so, it opens up a series of possible futures. It lets us imagine what the world would be like if things were a little different—or sometimes a great deal different. It takes us out of our comfort zones and lets us see the world in a new way.

It is, as such, a revolutionary book, encouraging, I hope, a taste for change, in a small way. Because if things can be different in the future—and they will be, we can be certain of that if of nothing else—then we might be able to look into the way that things actually happen in the real world, and plan things differently.

INTRODUCTION

But it is not just revolutionary, because all these speculations also carry within them a serious warning. Change never comes just by itself. It carries a whole range of peculiar side-effects and unexpected secondary shifts that might have been impossible to predict if it wasn't for our economists. The law of unintended consequences has been unleashed here and we can see what it means on nearly every page.

"Give me a one-handed economist!" exclaimed President Woodrow Wilson, complaining about the way that his economists used to answer his questions with the phrase "on the one hand... on the other hand... ." That is what unintended consequences mean, but it is also true that traditional economists have tended to guard their predictions with a whole series of qualifications that might protect them if things turn out differently.

The economists writing here, looking at a range of questions—from the nature of money to the environmental limits of the earth—are all one-handed, in the sense that they are straightforward, they mean what they say, and they don't beat around the bush. You may not agree with them— and sometimes they don't agree with each other—but what you will get is an unambiguous prediction or speculation about the future and the way the universe stacks up when it comes to money, cause by intricate cause.

So I hope that, by dipping into the pages that follow, readers might be able to recapture the pioneering spirit of economics, when people like Adam Smith set out with their notebooks and calculating machines and interpreted the world—as it was and as it might be in the future.

David Boyle

MONEY

INTRODUCTION
MONEY

The Venetian traveler Marco Polo introduced a chapter in his book on China with these words: "How the Great Kaan Causeth the Bark of Trees, Made Into Something Like Paper, to Pass for Money All Over His Country." Polo marveled at the banknotes he had seen and described how they worked, enforced by the will of the Great Khan himself. There was no question of whether or not you should accept one of his paper notes—the Great Khan demanded it.

These days, economists describe the kind of money that exists because those in authority say it does as "fiat" currency, using the word borrowed from the beginning of the Book of Genesis (*fiat lux*, "Let there be light"). But then, these days the business of understanding money, let alone defining it, would make Marco Polo's head spin. About $4 trillion circulates around the world every day, most of it speculation. Around 97 percent of the money in circulation is not made up of coins, or even of the banknotes that Marco Polo saw; it is made up of the bytes and bytes and bytes of information that circulate electronically.

We have gone from a period when money was underpinned by gold sitting underneath the vaults of the Bank of England or the Federal Reserve of New York City, which has looked after much of the world's gold reserves since World War II, to a period when nothing is quite what it seems. For example, now that money is no longer metal or paper, but information, there is almost no limit to how much you can store. It also means that debits and credits are very much the same: they are computer blips, and they are regarded as prized assets by those who hold them.

That slow shift in the form that money takes raises a whole range of questions, and our authors wrestle with some of them in this chapter. What if everyone was rich? What if we wiped the slate clean and everyone started from scratch with no debts? What if gold was worth peanuts or money grew on trees? The chapter also looks at some of the peculiarities in the way we use money today—should we all have one international currency, or would that cause curious side effects in the difference between rich and poor? Should we all have our own local currencies, or would that have peculiar side effects, too? You can test your answers against those of the experts here.

WHAT IF WE WERE ALL RICH?

Tim Leunig

 Being rich is both an absolute and a relative concept. I am rich because I have enough food to eat, decent accommodation—and so on. Many readers of this book will be in the same fortunate circumstances. It would be possible for all of us to be rich in this sense. But being rich is also a relative concept. You could say the rich are those who own paintings by Picasso, who have houses in fabulous locations, such as overlooking Central Park in New York. It is impossible for all of us to be rich in that sense, because these goods or opportunities are finite. A world in which everyone was very rich, and equally rich, would see different people live differently according to their tastes, but all equally well. Those who preferred fine art to speedboats would have the fine art, but not the speedboat. If more people wanted to live overlooking Central Park, skyscrapers around the park would grow taller, and, failing that, other desirable locations would spring up. The ultimate expression of being rich is often to have servants. Yet if everyone is rich, the wages of servants will be very high, and the rich will not be able to afford to hire them for more than a token amount of time. This means that servants' work will largely be mechanized. This has already happened to a large extent: washing machines, tumble dryers, and dishwashers are standard in middle-class homes, so that few people feel the need for a full-time servant. Battery-powered robotic vacuum cleaners that can clean an entire floor on their own, before returning to base to recharge, are becoming more common. Self-cleaning glass will replace too-expensive-to-hire window cleaners, and the same sort of technology will be applied to the inside of baths and other similar areas.

What Then?

By historical standards almost everybody in the world is rich. 200 years ago, few if any people in the world had adequate access to all the following—food, safe drinking water, proper sanitation facilities, health care, shelter, and at least a primary-level education. Today five out of six people have these things, and the proportion is growing rapidly. There are people alive now who will probably see the day in which no one meets the classic definition of absolute poverty.

What Gives?

13 Domestic servants as percentage of the working population in the UK in 1900.

0.4 Domestic servants as percentage of the working population in Canada in 2008.

11 Domestic servants as a percentage of the working population in Saudi Arabia in 2008.

What Else?

What if there was no such thing as money? *See page 24*

What if we all earned the same? *See page 46*

WHAT IF MONEY GREW ON TREES?

Tony Greenham

 In a sense, money once did grow on trees. In medieval England the king paid his bills with sticks. Hazelwood sticks had notches cut down one side to show the amount owed, and were then split down the middle so that one half could be used to prove the other was genuine. These "tally sticks" were really just a promise from the king—an IOU. People were happy to accept them for payment because they knew they could use them later on to pay their taxes. Tally sticks were used in many countries, and remained in circulation until the 19th century. Many other items have also been used as money, including large stones on the Micronesian island of Yap. Paper money was first introduced in 7th-century China. Some forms of money, such as gold coins, are valuable in themselves, but tally sticks and paper banknotes are examples of money as a token. If these tokens do not grow on trees, and are not dug out of the ground, then where do they come from? Today, most money is digital in the form of the balances in our bank accounts. But we do not own the deposits in our accounts. Just like the tally sticks, it is a promise to pay, but this time from our banks rather than the king. When the banking system makes more loans, it creates more promises to pay and so increases the amount of money. If too much money is created relative to the amount of exchanging and investing that is happening in the economy, the money will lose its value. But if too little is created, the economy will suffer falling investment and higher unemployment. So it does not matter what money is made of. What matters is how much money is circulating in the economy and how confident we are in its value. We would not be very confident in the value of leaves. As historian Niall Ferguson says, "Money is not metal. It is trust inscribed."

What Then?

If money really did grow on trees there would be no control over the amount of money in circulation. It would rapidly lose value in a process called hyperinflation. We would no longer trust it to keep its value and so people would refuse to accept it as payment. This happened in Germany in the 1920s and trust was restored only by introducing a completely new currency that was backed by the USA.

What Gives?

$85 trillion
Total amount of money in the world.

100 quintillion
The highest denomination banknote ever issued. The 100-quintillion pengő note was issued in Hungary in 1946. 100 quintillion has 20 zeros after the 1.

700 years The period
of time that tally sticks were in use in England.

What Else?

What if money obeyed the laws of thermodynamics? *See page 22*

What if there was no such thing as money? *See page 24*

WHAT IF WE WIPED THE SLATE CLEAN?

Tony Greenham

 Under ancient Hebrew law every 50th year was a jubilee year. Debts were forgiven, slaves freed, and lands restored to their original inhabitants. Similarly, in the ancient civilization of Babylonia, "clean slate" edicts canceled debts and allowed debtors to return to land that had been seized for nonpayment of debts. This practice helped preserve economic order because in these societies poor harvests could lead to farmers' debt and interest payments reaching levels beyond their ability to pay. Seizing their land and depriving them of their income was self-defeating. Allowing debtors to return to land they historically cultivated was easier when land was viewed as being held in common, or belonging ultimately to God, and therefore unavailable to be permanently bought or sold. The accumulation of interest was also thought to give an unfair share of wealth to lenders at the expense of those tending crops. In recent times, the Jubilee 2000 Campaign persuaded the world's richest countries to cancel some of the debts owed to them by the world's poorest. Releasing poor countries from burdensome debt payments, it was argued, would allow them to become more prosperous—and everyone would benefit in the end. More general debt relief might similarly require the richest in society to give up some of their wealth now to promote greater future prosperity for all. Wiping the slate clean was necessary in premodern times because economies did not grow. If your income grows consistently every year, it is far easier to service and increase your debt. Rapid economic growth since the Industrial Revolution has certainly made debt less of a problem than it was for the Babylonians. However, some argue that ecological pressures will mean much slower growth in future. If so, we might rediscover the benefits of debt cancellations as a solution to the buildup of unrepayable debts.

What Then?

Debt cancellation creates the danger of encouraging irresponsible behavior. Economists call this "moral hazard." What if people just went on a spending spree and got straight back into debt, expecting never to have to repay? Would all those who avoided borrowing feel it was unfair for debtors to be let off the hook? Debt cancellations might be the right thing to do in some circumstances, but they are by no means an easy answer.

What Gives?

$120 billion
Poor country debt canceled as a result of the Jubilee 2000 campaign.

$966 billion
Total balance of student loans in the USA.

$109,000 billion
Total global debt in 2010, including households, businesses, and governments—up 91 percent in 10 years from 2000.

What Else?

What if the economy stopped growing? *See page 78*

What if there was no interest charge? *See page 80*

WHAT IF MONEY OBEYED THE LAWS OF THERMODYNAMICS?

Tony Greenham

We do not think of money as being connected with the laws of physics, but some economists have suggested that it should be. Money can grow indefinitely through the accumulation of compound interest. It is also indestructible in the sense that it does not degrade over time. This makes money different from everything else found in Nature, which is ruled by the laws of thermodynamics. The first law states that energy and matter cannot be created out of nothing, but only transformed from one state to another. The second law observes that each time energy and matter are transformed they become less useful. So why does this matter? Finding a permanent store of value is difficult in the natural world—food degrades, metal rusts, and stone crumbles. Even land must be tended to maintain its productivity. Economic production is governed by the laws of thermodynamics. In contrast, money does not degrade. There is nothing in Nature that can grow forever, but money left in an interest-bearing account will do just that. For these reasons, some economists have suggested that money should "rust," or reduce in value over time by having a handling cost or negative interest rate applied to it. Currencies like this were introduced in the USA and Europe during the Great Depression of the 1930s. Local governments and chambers of commerce issued vouchers that could be spent like normal cash, but to remain valid they had to have a postage stamp fixed on them each week. These vouchers circulated very quickly, with people even paying their taxes early. This reinvigorated the local economy and got people back to work. However, central banks and governments took a dim view of these 'stamp scrip" currencies, and outlawed their use.

What Then?

Negative interest rates would change the way we think of and use money, which would no longer be a store of value. Money would be used only for transactions, as a convenient means of exchanging goods and services. To build up long-term savings for the future we would instead have to invest in real assets such as shares, bonds and loans, land and buildings, or even precious metals or fine art.

What Gives?

4,000 Number of stamp scrip currencies launched in the USA during the Great Depression.

What Else?

What if there was no such thing as money? *See page 24*

What if there was no interest? *See page 80*

WHAT IF
THERE WERE NO SUCH
THING AS MONEY?

Tony Greenham

What is money? This question is more difficult than it seems. Economists usually try to answer it by describing what money does. It is used as a common unit of account, a store of value, and a means of exchange. But this does not really answer the question because many different commodities have been used to fulfill these functions, from cowrie shells in premodern times to cigarettes in prisons today. In fact, it is not even necessary to use a commodity at all; many thousands of years ago, the societies of ancient Mesopotamia were recording transactions on clay slabs without money physically changing hands. So money can be thought of not as a commodity, but more as a promise to pay, or a social relationship. Money is a reciprocal relationship because for everything we give away in a market, such as time working for an employer, we expect to receive an equal value back in the form of someone else's labor or products. Not all social relationships are like this, of course. Throughout history communities operated without money in a gift economy rather than a market economy. In a gift economy we give the fruits of our labor to others to meet their needs. We are happy to do this because we are confident that others will do the same to ensure that our own needs are met. There is no need to use money to keep score. This degree of trust is possible in small, strongly connected social groups or extended families, but difficult with people we do not know. We can still exchange with strangers without using money, as long as we can barter directly with them. This requires us both to have something that the other desires. In trades of simple goods this might be possible, but in a modern economy many goods and services are produced by many different people all carrying out particular specialized jobs.

What Then?

Without money we would have to give freely to others, trusting that others would willingly cater for our own needs. Many have dreamed of such a world, and some successfully live in small communities on this basis. Such communities still need to trade with other communities, and it is hard to see how the large-scale industrial production and highly specialized jobs needed to produce computers and pharmaceuticals, say, would be possible under such a system.

What Gives?

20 Percentage of international trade carried out by direct exchange without using money.

75 United Nations' estimate of percentage of work carried out by women—for only 10 percent of the pay.

What Else?

What if money grew on trees?
See page 18

What if the government gave everyone enough money to live on?
See page 50

HISTORICAL
WHAT IF WE JUST KEEP PRINTING BANKNOTES?

Printing more money got a bad name for itself early on. The printed notes that Scottish adventurer John Law used to replace the French national debt in 1716 created such mayhem in Parisian society that they are often blamed for causing the French Revolution two generations later. Printed money also fueled the American Revolution, although the state of Massachusetts had been printing money since the 1690s.

"This currency, as we manage it, is a wonderful machine," said Founding Father Benjamin Franklin, a great enthusiast for printed money, at the height of the American War of Independence. "It performs its office when we issue it; it pays and clothes troops, and provides victuals and ammunition; and when we are obliged to issue a quantity excessive, it pays itself off by depreciation." Franklin put his finger on the real problem. This business of depreciation can be a downside of oiling the wheels of the economy. Too much money chasing too few goods will cause inflation and, if there is too much money in circulation, its value will drop.

Sometimes the inflation becomes catastrophic. The hyperinflation that hit Weimar Germany for three years from 1921 is usually blamed on the decision to finance the German war effort in World War I by borrowing, but it was the payment of reparations to the victorious Allies that tipped the balance. The value of the mark went from 60 marks to $1 to a terrifying 4,200,000,000,000 marks for the same amount.

This extreme situation—the complete collapse of belief in the value of money—famously led to people pushing wheelbarrows full of notes through the streets to buy a loaf of bread, only to find they could no longer afford it by the time they reached the end of the queue. By the close of 1923, a pound of bread cost 3 billion marks, a pound of meat cost 36 billion marks, and a single glass of beer cost 4 billion marks.

The Weimar inflation was only cured by a new currency, introduced in 1923, linked to the value of gold. Similar problems have hit a number of other countries, ranging from Hungary and Poland to North Korea and Israel. Most recently, and most disastrously, inflation reached 624 percent a year in Zimbabwe in 2004.

Inflation can ruin a society. Most historians believe the hyperinflation in Weimar Germany so undermined the nation's institutions that it paved the way for Adolf Hitler to seize power a decade later. Inflation wipes out the value of savings and debts. For a time, it can benefit people who are in debt, wiping out the value of the money they owe. But then even they begin to suffer as goods become scarce and their incomes dwindle in value as well.

Yet not all printed money has this effect. Money has to come from somewhere, after all, and most of it is created—in effect, printed—by commercial banks in the form of mortgages and loans. If those loans go to productive businesses that increase the amount of work going on in the economy, prices will probably stay steady. If they go on consumerism or speculation, then that will be inflationary.

So the key issue is not so much whether to crank up the printing machine. Sometimes you have to do that when the means of exchange runs short. Central bankers tend to call it something more polite such as "quantitative easing." The real issue is how the money you print is going to be used.

WHAT IF GOLD WERE WORTH PEANUTS?

David Boyle

Imagine that we woke up one morning and found that somebody had discovered how to make gold out of sugar—or sand, or even dust. The dream of alchemists for generations might finally have been achieved, but it would be a worrying day for investors—and for the governors of central banks. Imagine finding that the store of wealth in your vault that underpinned your nation's ability to borrow money was suddenly worthless. If gold was worth peanuts, then peanuts would be all you would get for your gold bars. How many peanuts would you need to find to provide collateral for the US national debt? This might not matter so much in times of plenty, when the world's reserve currencies are riding high, and the value of gold is low and matters much less. But if it happened when investors were using gold as a way to preserve the value of their wealth, and central bankers were clinging to their gold reserves for security in difficult times, what then? We might expect panic on the world markets as lenders hurried to find how much the value of gold was guaranteeing their loans to governments. If gold was uncertain, everything would be uncertain—and the world markets would be likely to demonstrate their skills at panic selling. And all from a scarce metal that pays no dividends and does nothing useful except sit in a vault, much of it under the Federal Reserve of New York City, which keeps most of the world's gold reserves to save on transportation costs. No wonder British economist John Maynard Keynes called gold a "barbarous relic."

What Then?

Having survived the shocking discovery that their precious gold investments were worth nothing, the world's investors would then have to answer another big question. Where should they put their money in the difficult times when other investments are unreliable? Old Masters or vintage wines? Van Goghs or vin rouge? Or should they fall back on tried and tested precious metals, and opt to play safe with silver?

What Gives?

215ft² (20m²)
Amount of gold ever mined in the world: a cube about the size of a duplex.

1999 Year in which the last country to link the value of its currency to gold, Switzerland, stopped doing so.

What Else?

What if money grew on trees?
See page 18

What if tulips were priceless?
See page 88

WHAT IF WE STARTED A WORLD CURRENCY?

Tony Greenham

A world currency could bring several benefits. International trade would be easier; the costs of changing currencies would be eliminated, as would the uncertainty of daily changes in exchange rates. Daily speculation in foreign exchange would become redundant. The boost to trade and greater efficiency of specialization of production should in theory make everyone better off. However, there are perils. Sharing the same currency means sharing the same interest rates. If the performance of economies diverges too much, it becomes hard to set interest rates that benefit all nations. Some economists argue that for a currency union to be successful there would have to be political or fiscal union, too. This would allow resources to be transferred from prosperous regions to poor areas. An alternative to a single world currency would be one that operated in parallel with national and local currencies. In 1944 British economist John Maynard Keynes and German-born economist/statistician E. F. Schumacher proposed a universal currency called Bancor to stabilize the international trade system. This would not replace national currencies, but international trade would take place within a mutual barter clearing system with each nation having to export enough to pay for its imports. Other currencies have often become a de facto world currency, and gold has always been acceptable. From the Roman aureus to the 20th-century US dollar, the international unit of account has effectively been set by the financial superpower of the day. In the 21st century the World Wide Web has given rise to private digital currencies, such as Bitcoin, that aim to be accepted for Internet trading across borders. The rise of new economic powers, such as China, Brazil, and India, has renewed calls for a new international currency that is truly shared between nations.

What Then?

A single world currency might require a single world government. However, a world currency like Bancor could be introduced for international trade without abolishing local currencies. One effect of this would be that nations that currently import much more than they export would have to reduce their consumption or compete harder in international markets. Exporting powerhouses would have to acquire more of a taste for the goods and services of other nations.

What Gives?

182 Number of different national currencies including the euro.

62 Percentage of official central bank foreign currency reserves held in US dollars.

£ The British pound sterling is the oldest currency still in use.

What Else?

What if we just kept printing banknotes? *See page 26*

What if we only imported things we couldn't make or grow ourselves? *See page 84*

WORK

INTRODUCTION
WORK

In 1932, British economist John Maynard Keynes wrote: "When we reach the point when the world produces all the goods that it needs in two days, as it inevitably will, we must turn our attention to the great problem of what to do with our leisure." Nor was he the only one to believe this. British science fiction writer Arthur C. Clarke talked about a near future in which "our descendants will be... faced with a future of utter boredom, where the main problem in life is deciding which of the several hundred TV channels to select."

It didn't turn out like that. This future was predicted by economists as late as the middle of the 20th century, so there has been a debate more recently about why they got it so wrong. Why didn't the endless leisure time for everyone stretching into the distance come true? In practice, Keynes and Clarke and the others were not wrong—they were inaccurate. The answer was much more complicated, because the work was never evenly spread—and the distribution became more uneven. There are some among the wealthiest people who don't need to work, and

many millions of the poorest for whom work is scarce—but in the middle, people work even more frenetically than before. Also, it wasn't that work became automated and scarce, although some did. What actually happened was that a great deal of work became unaffordable—companionship or care for the elderly is still work that needs doing, but it is hard to find the money to pay for it. In addition, work was viewed simplistically by some economists, who saw earning money as the only motivation for working, and found the idea of people working for less because it was inspiring or ethical difficult to comprehend.

Work remains a challenge to understand in its human diversity, so the questions we ask in this section are equally diverse and just as challenging—and they are important questions, too. What if nobody wanted to work any more? What if people only worked at the weekend and rested during the week? What if teachers were paid huge sums and bankers had to scrabble around for enough to pay the rent? All these are important questions for all our futures—and the answers are here. Read on to see if you agree with them.

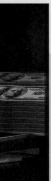

WHAT IF WORK WERE FUN?

Ruth Potts

Economists have generally approached work as necessary to "earn" leisure. But what if work itself could be satisfying? Addressing the scourge of "insane work" in 1974, German-born economist E. F. Schumacher wrote: "Dante, when composing his vision of hell, might well have included the mindless, repetitive boredom of working on a factory assembly line. It destroys initiative and rots brains." Forty years on, fewer of us are in factories, but the logic of the assembly line has leached into almost every aspect of working life. The result: we spend more and more time at work (by 2000, two-adult households in the USA had added 11 hours to their combined weekly workload since 1969) with progressively less scope to shape what we do. Surveys show a plummeting proportion of people who report that they have much influence over their daily working lives. Neither did people skip merrily to Henry Ford's assembly lines. As American writer and strategist turned motor mechanic Matthew Crawford explains, before the factory line accustomed people to that kind of alienation, they tended to choose vocation over a higher wage. So perhaps it could be different? Schumacher believed that good work was essential to a good life. His Buddhist perspective suggested that work should have three functions: to give people a chance to use and develop their faculties; to enable people to overcome egocentrism by joining with others in common tasks; and to "bring forth the goods and services needed for a becoming existence." If work was fun, we wouldn't need to live for the weekend because every day would be good. Mega-bonuses would vanish if our jobs were their own reward. Perversely, we might work less if we actually enjoyed what we did. We would certainly spend a good deal less on therapy, whether of the retail variety or the kind we get on the therapist's couch.

What Then?

Caring for people, perfecting a craft, or performing a concerto are naturally disobedient to the test of an accountant's profit: speed up a symphony and the result is cacophony. If work was fun, we could value what we do. Develop the human element by focusing on quality, not quantity, and we could share the work we have a little better. Satisfied, we would need to buy less 'stuff" to make us happy.

What Gives?

1913 American industrialist Henry Ford installs the first assembly line for the production of an entire motorcar.

12.8 Percentage fall—from 60 percent to 47.2 percent—between 1987 and 2012 in the number of Americans satisfied with their jobs.

Top 5 According to the University of Chicago, the five "happiest jobs" are: clergymen/women, firefighters, physical therapists, authors, and special education teachers.

What Else?

What if we all earned the same?
See page 46

What if we stopped buying stuff?
See page 92

WHAT IF
THE WORKING WEEK
WERE THREE DAYS LONG?

Andrew Simms

 Why is a five-day week the norm for many people? In the Netherlands a four-day week is already a standard and popular option whether you work in a school, bank, or hospital. From Utah in the USA to public offices in The Gambia, people are experimenting with working shorter hours, so the issues have already been wrestled with, whether these are to do with childcare or the basic affordability of working less. In both the Netherlands from the early 1990s and Utah after the financial crisis of 2008, the experiment in having a shorter working week began in the public sector. Flexibility proved key. Government departments in Utah went down to a four-day week, but worked longer hours on the other days. More than 80 percent of employees thought it improved working life and their well-being, only 3 percent said it made childcare harder and around 33 percent of members of the public thought access to services improved. It cut carbon emissions, too. Working shorter hours in the Netherlands is supported by much better state-supported childcare, making it easier for women to work; one in three Dutch men also work shorter or compressed hours. Instead of working ever longer in response to economic problems, many more could follow examples of people working less and differently. The past suggests nothing is set. In some medieval periods, people worked fewer days than in the modern age. Yet during the Industrial Revolution, only in 1825 was child labor limited to 12 hours on a week day and nine hours on Saturday, and some believed that a half-day off at the weekend would cause "immorality." Shorter working weeks could help solve the twin problems of major structural unemployment and overwork. More time at home could be good for neighborhoods, the environment, and our personal health and well-being.

What Next?

Changes to reduce the number of hours worked per week could be widely introduced right now if flexibly applied. Workplaces might offer all new employees the choice of working so-called "compressed hours," fewer but longer days or simply fewer hours. This would accommodate the wide range of circumstances in which employers and employees find themselves. It could be called National Gardening Leave; willing workplaces could simply sign up to offer the choice.

What Gives?

14 percent Fall in carbon emissions when Utah's state government put its workers on a four-day week.

15 Number of hours a week British economist John Maynard Keynes predicted people would be working by 2000.

What Else?

What if we retired at 30?
See page 48

What if well-being was the main purpose of economics?
See page 112

WHAT IF JOBS CAME FIRST?

Helen Kersley

Along with satisfying personal relationships and good health, a job is near the top of the list of things people care most about. Jobs are also high on the agenda for politicians. Even so, our principal measure of economic success is not jobs, but rising Gross Domestic Product (GDP)—the total of production/spending in the economy. Our economic model has it that job creation comes through strong GDP; and typically when GDP is rising, employment also rises. However, even in the good times before the post-2007 downturn, many economies were not succeeding in providing enough jobs (let alone ones providing adequate income and decent conditions). Research shows that having meaningful work isn't just important for meeting material needs but also plays a major part in people's health, fulfillment, and well-being. On the other hand, unemployment—especially long-term unemployment—is associated with poorer health and social outcomes, costly both to individuals and society. The importance of jobs for people is somewhat at odds with the operation of our economic system. The system strives for efficiency and profit involving an endless search to increase production and reduce costs, including the wage bill, either through lower salaries or fewer workers. The effect is that unemployment tends to rise and wages tend to fall, and these costs have to be carried by individuals, communities, and the state. What would happen if we replaced the existing model with one in which success was primarily measured in terms of the quantity and quality of jobs? This would be to treat jobs formally as a benefit and not just a cost. It could start a shift to policies, activities, and resources devoted to supporting employment. If success was to be measured in jobs, we would have to look at the quality too—to make sure that the jobs were good enough and worth doing.

What Then?

What we measure tends to drive incentives and effort. So if economic success was gauged primarily by jobs and not just growth, incentive structures would alter significantly. The result should be more resources directed to jobs rather than short-term profit or financial return, implying a more equal sharing of wealth generated by the economy and society. It might even lead to a new definition of wealth altogether, in which human returns counted more equally alongside financial ones. However, if we were not careful, it could also lead to increased inefficiency.

What Gives?

600 million Number of new jobs required globally in the 15 years after 2013.

11 Average percentage rate of unemployment in the 27 nations of the European Union.

24 Average percentage rate of youth unemployment in the 27 nations of the European Union.

What Else?

What if money grew on trees? *See page 18*

What if we were paid what we are worth? *See page 44*

WHAT IF TEACHERS WERE PAID MORE THAN INVESTMENT BANKERS?

Helen Kersley

 According to economic forecasters, one of the key trends shaping the future world of work is the need for more highly skilled workers and fewer unskilled workers. The forecasters advise nations and individuals to invest heavily in "human capital," including education and training for intellectual and technological skills. If higher academic achievement in knowledge-based skills is a priority for future prosperity, good teachers should be at a premium. Perhaps if anyone were to receive a seven-figure salary, it would better be a teacher than an investment banker. However, one important question is: should anyone be earning rewards in the many hundreds of thousands or millions? Can society afford it? Take public finances. With a high proportion of education provided publicly around the world, paying teachers more than investment bankers would certainly stretch fiscal limits. In England, for example, there are around 430,000 teachers in state-run schools. If just the top 10 percent each received £1 million in remuneration per year like some of the top investment bankers, then the bill would amount to about three-quarters of the entire budget for education in 2011–12. Public finances aside, there is still the question of whether society can really afford for anyone to earn such astronomical sums. Top bankers' salaries are justified on the basis that these individuals make huge profits for their companies and deserve to take a cut. But the profits themselves depend on the finance sector being in such a dominant position in the economy as to be able to extract a disproportionate share of economic value, including through unproductive, casino-style activities. Banking has a critical role to play in the economy—by lending to businesses, for example—but it is not this type of activity that has driven the astronomical salaries.

What Then?

If teachers were paid more than investment bankers, we could expect more people to seek a career in teaching. One argument is that this would create a bigger pool of talent from which to select the best teachers. However, financial incentivizing might not lead so simply to the best. Teachers need to be well remunerated for doing such important and demanding work, but other factors matter for excellent teaching—such as support, teamwork, and social esteem.

What Gives?

$39,000 Average
salary for a teacher with 15 years' experience across countries in the OECD.

$320,000
Average pay for staff in investment banks globally, but top bankers can earn multimillion dollar sums.

What Else?

What if work was fun?
See page 36

What if we were paid what we are worth? *See page 44*

WHAT IF WE WERE PAID WHAT WE ARE WORTH?

Helen Kersley

We are used to people earning vastly different wages for different jobs. The pay and benefits of top chief executives, for example, are typically several million pounds a year, whereas a teacher's assistant might expect to earn about $25,000. But how confident are we that wages truly reflect how worthwhile various occupations are? How much do we depend on the individuals doing particular jobs? How much do they improve our lives? We have probably experienced directly the value of a nurse or a plumber, but what about less direct relationships—civil servants or marketing professionals, say? There are challenging complexities here, but questioning worth is worthwhile. Some city financiers still take stratospheric sums in pay even after their activities created the worst economic crisis since the 1930s Great Depression. The general idea is that pay rewards productivity, such as how much money we make for our company. That doesn't tell us a lot about how valuable the activity of an individual or company is to society at large, however. An activity might be helping create jobs and a better quality of life, or it might be environmentally unsustainable or causing local businesses to fold. In reality the pay–productivity relationship is quite tenuous. More decisive is negotiating power. Think of the power of senior executives in achieving rapid escalation in their pay, despite this being unmatched by achievements in company performance. If pay depended more on worth we would question the positive and negative outcomes of different occupations. Organizations would need to account for their "externalities": the costs they create but don't pay for (for example, pollution or job losses), and alternatively the benefits they create but for which they are not rewarded (for example, protection of land or positive community relations). Fully reflecting worth should incentivize more socially good outcomes and less bad or risky ones.

What Then?

Rewarding the activities of companies, institutions, and individuals according to their broad worth could shift activities in the economy and society quite fundamentally. In terms of economic theory, this should help markets work better because more information means less market failure. Getting it absolutely right would be challenging but new ways of measuring the results of everything that happens, not just money, might be a good start.

What Gives?

$31:$1 Ratio of chief executive to average worker pay in the top 500 US companies, 1970.

$325:$1 Ratio of chief executive to average worker pay in the top 500 US companies, 2008.

What Else?

What if we were all rich?
See page 16

What if teachers were paid more than investment bankers?
See page 42

WHAT IF
WE ALL EARNED
THE SAME?

Tim Leunig

There is a famous story told to all economics students that explains why the world would be a worse place if we all earned the same. Let's imagine that we did, in fact, all earn the same. I earn my living from writing, tennis players from hitting a ball, and singers from singing. We all earn the same, and the law says that none of us can earn any more than the other. Imagine that this weekend Novak Djokovic, Roger Federer, and Adele have spare time. I would love to see Djokovic and Federer battle it out on court, before going to spend the evening at an Adele concert. But since the three of us already earn the same amount, this can only happen if I can persuade them to perform free of charge. After all, if I pay them, they will earn more than me, and that is not allowed. Perhaps more seriously, if we all earned the same, there would be no incentive to work hard at school. After all, you will earn the same however many qualifications you have. Going to college would be a particularly bad idea, since you would earn nothing while at college, and then still earn the same as you would have done in any case. There would also be no incentive to work hard in a job—as getting promoted brings no financial reward. Waiters could be as surly as they liked, as tips would be banned. Indeed, why bother to show up on time, since you are guaranteed the same wage as everyone else? There would be no incentive to invent anything, as you would not be allowed to make any money from it. Inequality—at least up to a point—turns out to be a price worth paying for the incentives it creates.

What Then?

Ben and Jerry's ice cream company once had the rule that no one could earn more than seven times the pay of the most junior employee. So the CEO, Ben, earned only seven times as much as the $8 an hour that entry-level employees earned. But of course Ben owned a big chunk of the company. The money he didn't pay himself ended up in the bank account of the company—which he owned!

What Gives?

$15,000 a year full-time
Minimum wage in the USA in 2012.

$4,200 a year full-time
Minimum wage in Algeria in 2012.

$35 million
Adele's annual earnings in 2012.

What Else?

What if we were all rich?
See page 16

What if we were paid what we are worth? *See page 44*

WHAT IF
WE RETIRED AT 30?

Tim Leunig

Broadly speaking, we start work at age 20, retire at 65, and die at around 90. So we work for around half our lives. For the first 20 years we are supported by our parents, which we repay by supporting our children in turn. We support ourselves as adults through work, and live off our savings when we retire. Working for half your life means that on average you must put aside half your income when you are working to pay for your children, or for your retirement. If you don't do that, you will have 45 glorious years, followed by a retirement begging on the street corner. That is not a lot of fun, so people save when they are working. They save in many ways—through savings accounts, private pensions, and by buying a house so that they can live rent- and mortgage-free when they retire. Even a government pension is saving in disguise: the government takes money from you as tax when you are working, and gives it back to you when you retire. Retiring at 30 would alter the balance between years spent working and years not working. Rather than having 45 of each, we would have 10 years working and 80 years not working. So each year we would have to put aside eight-ninths of our income to cover the years in which we did not work. The average person in a developed country earns around $40,000, so they would have to put aside $35,000 and live on the remaining $5,000. It is possible to live on $5,000 a year—it is the standard of living of a typical family in the Philippines or India. And that is the choice: you can work for 45 years and live well or you can work for 10 years and live in what most people reading this book would think of as poverty. People the world over prefer work to poverty, which is why only the very richest get to retire at 30.

What Then?

Retiring at 30 would mean big problems for the rest of the economy. Many companies would go bankrupt, because people would be spending less money on things. The government wouldn't get enough money in taxes from income taxes, sales taxes, or company taxes to pay for good roads, police, or schools. They also wouldn't be able to pay off the national debt. Even the leisure industry would suffer, as people would have little money to pay for vacations.

What Gives?

6.8 billion Total world population in 2013.

1.1 billion World population aged 20–30 in 2013.

52 Percentage of the world's population aged under 30 in 2013.

What Else?

What if the working week was three days long? *See page 38*

What if nobody wanted to work any more? *See page 52*

HISTORICAL
WHAT IF THE GOVERNMENT GIVES EVERYONE ENOUGH MONEY TO LIVE ON?

Giving everyone enough money to live on was the great radical dream of the Great Depression of the 1930s, and the result of a strange mixture of socialism, a hatred for the banks, and a fondness for the medieval guild system. It was known as social credit and was the brainchild of British engineer Clifford Hugh Douglas, who warned that there wasn't enough money in the world to pay back all the outstanding debts.

He wanted the government to stop banks from creating money, and to create instead in the form of a basic income for every citizen, credited to their account every month, which would "trickle up" the economy rather than "trickle down" as it was usually supposed to do.

By the 1930s, Douglas was able to fill stadiums with his supporters, especially in Australia and Canada. An estimated 90 million tuned into his radio broadcasts in the USA, and two Canadian states elected social credit administrations. A social credit administration stayed in power in Alberta until 1971, prevented by the courts from pushing through their promised C$25 dividend per person a month. In Britain, a breakaway wing of the Boy Scouts known as Kibbo Kift formed itself into the Social Credit Party and marched in green uniform as the Greenshirts. The party wound itself up in 1950, by which time the social credit movement had begun to be taken over by cranks and extremists, as radical movements so often are.

Social credit never happened and Douglas died, embittered, in 1952. Since then, there have been various attempts to create a basic "citizen's income," paid for out of taxes, and enough debate to be able to guess what might happen if it were introduced. First, taxes would be extremely high. Second, there would be a huge gulf between "citizens" who received the money and illegal immigrants or "noncitizens" who didn't. Third, there should be major savings in the welfare and tax system. Fourth, the whole salary system would have to change. If you had to persuade people to get out of bed to do jobs such as cleaning and garbage collection when they already had enough money to live on, those salaries would have to go up considerably.

More recently, governments have tried to use the welfare system to top up salaries to a basic income level, and here there is a famous historical precedent: Speenhamland. This was a welfare system devised by magistrates in 1795 in Speenhamland, Berkshire, southern England, to tackle poverty caused by high bread prices. The system topped up the wages of poor families so that they could afford to eat, and effectively reduced malnutrition. Unfortunately, it also allowed farmers to go on paying wages that were far too low, which meant that the scheme became increasingly expensive to administer.

In the years that followed, Speenhamland became a byword for economic inefficiency and was used by campaigners to create an alternative welfare mechanism, and described as "a universal system of pauperism." After the 1830s, the Speenhamland system was replaced by a network of workhouses in every parish for people who could not support themselves.

So there is the answer. If the government topped up wages to provide people with a basic income, as they do in so many places around the world, the danger is that wages would be kept artificially low. Then again if they simply paid a basic income to everyone, it might set people free to be and do what they most wanted. Yet it would only work if it was affordable, if the money in the economy was kept steady, and if people could be persuaded to do the dirty jobs that nobody wanted.

WHAT IF NOBODY WANTED TO WORK ANYMORE?

Tim Leunig

Virtually no one wants to work as it is. That's why employers have to pay their employees to show up. Pay is compensation for giving up your time. The less people like the work, the more you have to pay them. Few people want to work nights—so employers have to pay more for jobs that involve night work. Few people want to clean sewers, so those people are generally better paid than others with similar skill levels. On the main shop floor, workers dislike jobs with no freedom and autonomy. Henry Ford found that out when he created the production line. The work was hard—but so was almost every other job in that era. What made Ford's job different was the sheer minute-by-minute relentlessness of it all. It turned out people didn't like that very much—and quit left, right, and center. Ford had to pay twice the prevailing wage to attract and retain staff. Today many companies go to great lengths to try to make work interesting. They need people to want to show up to work. Otherwise absenteeism will rise in the short run, and in the long run wages will have to rise to compensate workers for the unpleasantness of the working environment. This is particularly true as a country develops, and more and more good jobs are available to workers. Things are a bit different at executive level. Executives don't want to work for companies that are considered antisocial. People want to work in industries that impress others. Today, that helps brands like Apple, and means that tobacco companies have to pay top dollar to attract good managers.

What Then?

If people became even less keen to work, wages would rise and it would be worth designing even more machines to replace workers. Computers would drive trains and planes, videos replace university faculty, and you would place your restaurant order by text message ("Two steaks for table 1: one rare, one medium"). Of course someone has to cook the food, but someone will take the job if wages are high enough.

What Gives?

20 Percentage of over-65s in the USA who still work.

10,000 a day
Number of "baby boomers" (people born 1946–64) retiring in the USA for the next 18 years.

36 Percentage of Americans saving nothing toward retirement.

What Else?

What if we retired at 30?
See page 48

What if everyone stopped buying stuff? *See page 92*

WHAT IF YOU NEEDED A PhD TO STACK SHELVES?

Helen Kersley

 The entry requirement for a host of occupations has been raised and narrowed since 1980, restricting access to many jobs to those with better academic qualifications, while reducing opportunities for nongraduates and others. Only a few decades ago, a career in journalism, for example, was open to those with respectable school grades. Now you need a degree and often a postgraduate qualification. As the job market has tightened, applications for entry-level jobs have become much more numerous—and will typically include those with higher degrees, even up to PhD level, as well as those with years of work experience. There seem to be two forces at work here. First, there are simply not enough jobs and our economic system seems chronically incapable of providing them. Second, educational achievement has become a primary means of sifting applicants, even if the job requires skills other than academic ones. That is not to say the PhD student will always get the one bar job available but, as the example of journalism shows, there is a discernible trend. So how far could this go? Could it be that by 2030, say, the only people who will be able to get a job will be those with the highest qualifications? What would the consequences be if you needed a doctorate to stack shelves? In the first place, restricting access to further parts of the labor market would exclude potential workers who do not continue education beyond high school. Then there is the possibility that we wouldn't be getting the best people into important jobs. Not everyone is able to reach high levels of academic achievement, or is interested in doing so, but some who do not may have a gift for dealing with people or may be manually dextrous. If we ignore these talents, we lose the diversity and creativity that a healthy, stable, and resilient society needs, not to mention security and well-being for a large share of the population.

What Then?

Education is expensive in time and money. If you needed the highest qualification to get even entry-level jobs then who, apart from those with family resources, would be able to afford college, masters degrees, and doctorates? This suggests an even more unequal world, and one of deep frustration—the frustration of those who have achieved academic heights but end up doing basic tasks at work, and the frustration of people who have no prospect of a job at all. It would seem like a toxic mix.

What Gives?

14.8 Percentage rate of youth unemployment (not in education, employment, or training) in the USA in 2011.

1,700 Number of applicants for eight job vacancies in a cafe in Nottingham, England, in 2013.

What Else?

What if work was fun?
See page 36

What if we were paid what we are worth? *See page 44*

PEOPLE

INTRODUCTION
PEOPLE

At the most recent turn of the century, a group of French economics students at La Sorbonne in Paris, France, organized their own revolt against their teachers and the way they were teaching economics and called it the Post-Autistic Economics campaign. "It was in the beginning a modest initiative, almost confidential," wrote French newspaper *Le Monde* in September 2000. "It has now become a subject of an important debate which has created a state of effervescence in the community of economists. Should not the teaching of economics in universities be rethought?"

The "post-autistic" campaigners argued that mathematics had "become an end in itself," turning economics into what they called an "autistic science," dominated by abstractions that bore no relation to the real world or to real people. Within two weeks, the petition calling for reconnection with the real world had 150 signatures, many from France's most important universities. Soon newspapers and TV stations all over France had picked up the story and even senior professors were starting a similar petition of their own. Soon the French education minister, Jack Lang, had promised to set up a commission to investigate.

By then, there had also been a vitriolic exchange of articles by French and American economists, a counterpetition launched by the Massachusetts Institute of Technology (MIT) in Cambridge, Massachusetts, and a peculiar post-autistic petition from PhD students at Cambridge University in England—unusual in that the signatories were too frightened for their future careers to put their real names to it.

The debate launched by the campaign suggested that economics was really about people, and not just about theorems, and that economists needed to learn from the way people actually behaved so they could see the world as it really is. But then that is what makes economics so fascinating, because—although it is certainly about people—it is also about how people interact, and especially how they interact with money and with each other's values. That is why economists are those who are so often called upon to predict things, especially when it comes to the outcomes of breakthroughs or initiatives.

WHAT IF "IRRATIONAL ECONOMIC WOMAN" REPLACED "RATIONAL ECONOMIC MAN"?

Ruth Potts

Although he never used the phrase, "rational economic man" is attributed to British philosopher and economist John Stuart Mill. He developed an analysis of man (woman) as a "being who desires to possess wealth and who is capable of judging the comparative efficacy of means for obtaining that end." Mill was clear that this was an abstraction, and of limited use, but the simplification proved irresistible. The idea of a "rational" actor responding to perfect information to maximize "utility" as a consumer and profit as a producer allowed economists to build models to predict (and then determine) economic outcomes. The problem is that people are pretty irrational. We shouldn't buy more food than we need and waste a third of it. Or repeat things that don't work, like buying more stuff in the belief that it will make us happy. But we do. How would "irrational economic woman" behave? Hungarian economic anthropologist Karl Polanyi documented the many societies in history that made choices based on reciprocity. New Zealand-born feminist economist Marilyn Waring revealed how economics excludes, and so fails to value, all the care that makes societies work. Behavioral economists show that we put too much weight on recent events; too little on future threats. Yet these advances only modify "economic man": freedom, justice, and care lie outside the realm of human behavior as far as economics is concerned. Using characteristics culturally construed as feminine might make economics more humane: we'd care about more than monetary wealth. American economist Julia Nelson suggests a return to an older definition of economics, as "the study of the ways societies organize themselves to provide for the survival and flourishing of life." Of course, nothing much might change. But surely, collectively, we can do better?

What Then?

"Irrational economic woman" isn't new, just unappreciated. Canadian economist Margaret Reid placed custodianship, care, and use at the heart of her "Household Economy," Marilyn Waring described economics "as if women counted" and American political economist Elinor Ostrom's work on common resources earned her an economics Nobel. Perhaps, the point is not to replace "man" with "woman" but to acknowledge the complex mix of characteristics that make humankind infinitely interesting—life might become more humane, and economics less miserable.

What Gives?

"UNPAID work makes all the rest of work possible."
New Zealand economist Marilyn Waring

"GOODS are produced for use, and returns are in use value rather than exchange value."
Canadian economist Margaret Reid

What Else?

What if there was such a thing as society? *See page 62*

What if women were in charge of finance? *See page 82*

WHAT IF THERE WERE SUCH A THING AS SOCIETY?

Ruth Potts

British prime minister Margaret Thatcher famously remarked that there is "no such thing as society." She believed that we are individuals, acting alone in the economy, and her policies—and the shape of the economy that followed—were based on that assumption. But what if she was wrong? What if economic policy were designed to support society rather than transform our souls, as she suggested it should? It would mean there would be encouragement for sharing resources, and discouragement for anything that prevented sharing—or got in the way of community life. There would be encouragement for informal caring. It would mean that economics would emphasize teamwork over individual leadership; it would study the way that groups worked together rather than just how they competed. And, after almost four decades of economic policymaking that operates on the assumption that we look after our own interests first, we remain remarkably collaborative. American author Rebecca Solnit traces numerous examples of people coming together in times of crisis that are more akin to the "beloved community" dreamed of by clergyman Martin Luther King Jr. than a Hobbesian nightmare (suggestive of the writings of English philosopher Thomas Hobbes, who believed that life was "nasty, brutish, and short"). Now a wave of new thinking in the natural sciences suggests that not only is Nature collaborative, but that this collaboration often outperforms competition—and that the two are, in any case, deeply involved with each other. There are those who argue that not believing in society encourages us to be suspicious, avaricious, and self-serving, leaving us unhappy and increasingly unequal. We also know that forcing people into community against their will can be destructive. Perhaps instead, we should learn to value the unique contributions we all make to wider society?

What Then?

If there is such a thing as society, we could prioritize policy that capitalizes on our social nature. Encouraging the gift economy nurtures the relationships that do most to enhance our well-being once basic needs are met. Value the social and we would spend less time in the office, and much more time contributing to our local communities. From growing food and sharing what we know to organizing street parties, life could be a lot more fun.

What Gives?

64.3 million
Number of Americans who did formal volunteering in their communities in 2011.

89.5 percent
Proportion of families in the USA who eat meals together more than once a week.

63.4 million
Number of people in the UK who are members of cooperatives (nearly the same as the whole population).

What Else?

What if "irrational economic woman" replaced "rational economic man"? *See page 60*

What if well-being was the main purpose of economics? *See page 112*

WHAT IF
WE FOUND A CURE
FOR CANCER?

Tony Greenham

 Increasing life expectancy has been one of the triumphs of human progress. In preindustrial England the average lifespan was under 40, and in ancient Rome less than 30. The most important change has been dramatic reductions in child deaths. In some of the world's poorest and most troubled regions, where as many as 18 of every 100 babies fail to see their fifth birthday, child mortality is still a major problem. But medieval Europe was much worse, with more than half of children dying before the age of five. We might not have found a cure for cancer, but modern medicine can successfully tackle a range of diseases that would have killed our ancestors. But how active and healthy will we be during these extra years, and who will look after us? Geographers and economists have developed indicators such as Healthy Life Years to track not just how long we live, but how long we live an active life. This matters not only for the quality of the life we lead, but also for how we provide for retirement and the care of those living with disabilities. We need enough people of working age to support those who are retired or otherwise unable to work. This is known as the dependency ratio, and it has been increasing steadily in many developed nations. When German Chancellor Otto von Bismarck introduced the world's first state pension in 1880, you had to reach 70 to collect it and life expectancy was only in the 40s. In contrast, a girl born today in Japan has a 50/50 chance of reaching 100 years old, but the official retirement age is only 60. However, many Japanese pensioners prefer to carry on working, at least part-time, because they find retirement dull. Whatever the future of medicine, we can expect to see more gray hairs at work.

What Then?

Finding a cure for cancer would not just reduce pain and suffering, it would also increase our average expected lifespans. We should hope that these extra years are healthy and active ones, otherwise the cost of medical treatment might increase rapidly. With rising life expectancies we might also need to accept that we work into our 70s instead of retiring in our 60s.

What Gives?

122 Longest confirmed lifespan of any person—Jeanne Calment of France, who died in 1997.

89 World's highest average life expectancy, in Monaco.

48 World's lowest average life expectancy, in Chad (central Africa).

What Else?

What if work was fun?
See page 36

What if we retired at 30?
See page 48

HISTORICAL
WHAT IF WE
ABOLISH SLAVERY?

The economic consequence of the abolition of slavery was the great unknown of the 19th century. What would happen when slavery was abandoned was a question debated bitterly by campaigners on both sides. And generations later historians still discuss the issue. Was abolition a decision of great generosity or an example of clever self-interest?

When the abolitionists first won a vote in the British House of Commons to abolish the slave trade in 1807, most educated people believed that it would be extremely costly. The decision for abolition had been made, not by economists, but by a campaign from mainly religious figures across the new evangelical movement. Britain had started the slave trade, taking slaves from Africa to the West Indies and the Americas, and bringing back tobacco and sugar from there to the ports at Liverpool and Bristol. It was Britain's trade and she could have continued to dominate it.

A powerful backlash, financed by the West Indies plantation owners, warned that the French and Spanish would take the slave trade over and profit by it. They eventually lost the argument and slavery was abolished in the British Empire in 1833, but the plantation owners won themselves a handsome £20 million in compensation.

On the face of it, abolition still looks like a brave decision, forced through because it was right and despite the loss of revenue. But historians more recently have pointed out that, from the 1770s, the West Indian plantations had been much less profitable, undercut by cheaper sugar from plantations in Brazil and Cuba. Once they had decided to abolish slavery, the British also lost no time trying to make sure nobody else profited by it either. The British navy patrolled the African coast, seizing slave ships bound for those rival plantations, until the trade had finally stopped.

Something else was going on with the economics of slavery: cotton. Advances in cotton production meant that the plantations still operating in the southern states of the USA began to become enormously profitable again. Throughout the early to mid-19th century, until the outbreak of the Civil War in 1861, the price of slaves—a key indicator—just kept rising: from up to $600 for a 30-year-old man in 1800 to up to $3,000 when the southern states tried to secede, far faster than inflation. Economists have estimated that owners in the south owned slaves worth $4 billion by 1860. That was a good economic reason for the war and some indication of what would happen when slavery was abolished.

When American economists Robert Fogel and Stanley Engerman wrote their controversial study *Time on the Cross* in 1974, using modern statistics to work out the profitability of slavery, they found that farms that used slaves were half as efficient again as farms that did not. The economics of slavery is borne out by what actually happened. The Deep South was impoverished by the Emancipation Declaration, but also by the deprivations imposed on them by the victors.

All this indicates that the decision to end the slave trade was exactly what it seemed—an economic sacrifice performed because it was right. But there is another way of looking at it. Recent evidence suggests that, because slaves were a profitable investment, they were usually looked after humanely by the owners. Despite this, very few freed slaves went back to their former masters for employment after they had been freed, even though they were worse off economically. Studies of the economics of slavery tend to miss out the crucial cost to the slaves themselves, in dignity and life opportunities and many other things, too.

Modern economics suggests that the argument is even more complicated than that. When people are made free and able to use their skills and imagination, then everyone profits. When they are not free, those skills are wasted. That is the answer to the big picture, looking back two centuries: we have all profited by the availability of the skills of generations of people who would otherwise have been slaves, and continue to do so today.

WHAT IF MARX WAS RIGHT?

David Boyle

 Unlike most economists, German philosopher Karl Marx set out very clearly in his writings exactly what he believed was going to happen. He predicted the imminent overthrow of the bourgeoisie by the proletariat; the end of private ownership of land, factories, or homes; and the takeover by the state of all credit, factories, transport—and a great deal else besides. Marx wasn't saying that this would be a good thing; he said it was inevitable. Yet it never happened. But if he was right after all, then his revolution still lies somewhere in the future. That would mean that a century and a half of welfare payments and consumerism, and a century and a half of efforts to humanize work—cutting hours and making sure a smaller proportion of the workforce gets mangled by machinery— would all have been in vain. It would mean that the rumblings of discontent will grow until the noise overwhelms the way the world is now arranged. It would mean that those who create the world's wealth, which is these days the poor, downtrodden factory workers of China and the Far East, will seize control of the means of production. It would mean that those who have become wealthy by financing them, the bankers of Wall Street and the City of London, will be set to work in factories and in the fields themselves. But then, Marx said a great deal in his career as a revolutionary, including the prediction that capitalism would eat away at traditions, nationalisms, loyalties, and relationships. "All that is sold melts into air," he stated. There, at least, Marx may well have been right after all.

What Then?

If the Marxist revolution were to come, the big question would be: how long will it last? Is centralized state planning the best, most effective, and most sustainable arrangement we can imagine? The evidence from Stalin's dominance over the Soviet Union in the middle years of the 20th century suggests it is actually one of the worst. Austrian-born British philosopher Karl Popper's book *The Open Society and its Enemies* suggested that that kind of society is also the least able to adapt.

What Gives?

34 percent
Highest communist vote share recorded in Europe—in Italy.

3.5 million Number
of people thought to have been sent to the gulag prison camps in Siberia by Stalin during his rule.

What Else?

What if there was such a thing as society? *See page 62*

What if well-being was the main purpose of economics? *See page 112*

WHAT IF
WE PAID PEOPLE
FOR HOUSEWORK?

Helen Kersley

 People living in Western societies generally share the understanding that work means going out into the economy to a job in business or services and getting paid. For those giving their labor for free, being an intern or volunteer is typically a precursor to a paid job. But what about all that activity that goes on in the home—caring for children and families, providing material and emotional sustenance, sorting out day-to-day events and challenges? These activities can be demanding and require long hours, but are they work? They meet vital immediate and long-term human needs, and free up the "real" workers to go out into the world and do their jobs. Yet they constitute unnamed work, invisible in the economy—unless, that is, you pay someone else to do them. Then they get a recognizable economic value, though not much. But in that case, the tasks being performed have not changed, only the person performing them. So if we are going to pay some people for these essential tasks, why not pay everyone who does them? In the UK, child benefit gives a minimal payment to many parents by the state. This is not earned income in the same way a wage from a job is. And it is definitely minimal—current rates for a parent with two children are pretty low in most places, and in the USA are just for poor people and are temporary. So, what if we paid people properly for their work in the home? It would give economic power and greater equality to millions of people, and women especially. It would allow those making a difference in the home to share some of the benefits. It would make us more aware how important that work is—rather than assuming that all wealth-creating is done in the conventional economy. And for people who work in the home, a change in pay status could mean a change in social status—fewer party conversations going cold, perhaps, when you respond to the question "What do you do?" with "I stay at home."

What Then?

Paying for "home" work would help bust the myth that nonmarket activity doesn't contribute to prosperity. It would demand that we broaden our recognition of what counts toward value. Paying for "home" work is bound to require major redistribution of income and profit through tax and benefit systems—no doubt deeply controversial. It could affect incentives and reshape much of our activity. And it could help reduce large and growing inequalities between people and communities. It would also be rather expensive.

What Gives?

$1/3-1/2$ Proportion of valuable economic activity in OECD countries accounted for by unpaid household production. Yet unpaid household production is not accounted for in traditional prosperity measures such as Gross Domestic Product (GDP) per capita.

What Else?

What if we were paid what we are worth? *See page 44*

What if we all earned the same? *See page 46*

WHAT IF WE LET ANYBODY LIVE ANYWHERE?

Tim Leunig

The USA let in unlimited numbers of European migrants during the 19th century. Millions moved, even though the passage to the United States was expensive and slow, and even though international migration in those days meant that you would almost certainly never see your family again, and might not even hear from them again. Today a flight is relatively cheap, and very fast. Letters, phone calls, email, texts, and face-to-face video calls on the Internet mean that you can keep in contact with friends back home. Given the opportunity, millions would move from poorer countries to richer countries, eager to work hard and make a better life for themselves. Today, after all, people are willing to risk their lives to enter the USA, Europe, or Australia. If we let anybody live anywhere, the first new migrants would probably be young men. If successful, they would bring their families and tell their friends. Migration would then snowball. If a sufficient number of people moved to one place, other would-be migrants might even be able to move and find work without speaking the home language. After all, if 20 million Chinese people moved to California, the next migrants from China would be able to get by without speaking English. Not everyone would move, however. Many people would have family or emotional ties to their home country, or would not have the confidence to try to build a new life from scratch. It is impossible to know how many people would move if everyone could live where they wanted, but it is very hard to imagine that fewer than 100 million would move, or more than 500 million. The Italian economy may not be doing well at present, but Italians like their country enough not to move en masse to better-performing Germany. Culture matters as well.

What Then?

In the very long term, people would move to places with better weather. People are already moving south within their own countries in every OECD country except Italy. A world of free movement would see few people in Canada, Northern Europe, or Russia, and far more people in the warmer parts of the temperate zones, such as California. Air conditioning makes hot, sunny countries very pleasant prospects—although that puts pressure on water supplies.

What Gives?

25 million Number of immigrants from Europe to the USA (1850–1930).

640 million Number of people worldwide who would like to move to another country, according to a 2012 poll.

$300 billion Annual remittances sent home by migrant workers worldwide.

What Else?

What if the world stopped flying? *See page 100*

What if money needed a passport to cross borders? *See page 124*

MARKETS

INTRODUCTION
MARKETS

Markets are absolutely everywhere, from city squares containing stalls of fruit and vegetables to the international currency and commodity exchanges, with their computer screens and tickertape figures. All our spending decisions involve us and create markets, but you may also find them in other places, too, whether it is decisions we take about the quickest way to get to work or even who washes the dishes in the family home. Just because no money changes hands, it doesn't rule out the possibility that market behavior is involved somewhere.

These other examples make it difficult to know how best to understand markets, and this is where economics has sometimes run into trouble in the past. Economists can understand exchanges and values—that is their core understanding—but they understand them that much better if they can incorporate some psychology (behavioral economics), some physics (econometrics), and perhaps some of the insights of ecology to see how the living systems of the Earth underpin our products and services.

Issues about markets dominate some of the basic divisions in political economy. Can markets be perfectly fair and effective if the peculiarities and irregularities are ironed out, or is such an ideal impossible in the real world? Are there better ways of allocating things between people according to what they want, or are these always going to be top-heavy and inefficient? Markets allow things to be given prices, but what if nobody can afford them?

These are the roots of the speculations you will find in this section—what if we only imported things we couldn't make or grow ourselves? What if people just stopped buying—and what if tulips were suddenly priceless? The advantage of asking about tulips is that we know the answer, because that is exactly what happened in the 17th-century Dutch Republic, and it was the very first recorded financial "bubble." For the answers to the other questions, you will have to test your predictions against those of our experts.

WHAT IF
THE ECONOMY
STOPPED GROWING?

Tony Greenham

 The massive growth in levels of production since the Industrial Revolution has enabled the consumption of goods and services on an unprecedented scale for over 1 billion people in developed countries. Rapid growth in developing countries holds the promise of delivering greater material prosperity to billions more. Economists measure the size of the economy by the financial value of production—known as Gross Domestic Product (GDP). We tend to assume that more GDP is always a good thing because it increases consumption, creates jobs, and allows governments to collect taxes to fund public services. However, GDP is not a good measure of human progress. It counts many activities that harm our welfare, such as crime, and omits other things that make life worthwhile—like liberty and friendship. It also counts the consumption of our planet's finite resources as income, while ignoring the costs of pollution and climate change. For these reasons the link between growth in GDP and improving living standards is weaker in rich countries than in developing nations. How the additional income is shared out is also important. If the gap between rich and poor gets wider, the economy could grow but still leave most people worse off. Classical economists of the 18th and 19th centuries thought that economic growth would eventually fade away once our material needs were satisfied, and that growth in consumption could not continue infinitely because natural resources are finite. However, they did not read into this an end to cultural, social, or scientific progress. Instead they thought that an economy that stopped growing, or reached a steady state, would allow us to focus less on what British economist John Maynard Keynes called the "disgusting morbidity" of accumulating wealth for wealth's sake and more on how to live "wisely and agreeably and well."

What Then?

Developments in technology make us more productive as time goes on, requiring less labor to produce the same amount. So in a steady state economy we would need gradually to reduce our working hours as we became more productive, to prevent unemployment rising. In order to allow poorer countries to continue to grow their material consumption to match levels in developed nations, we would all have to use natural resources much more efficiently.

What Gives?

11.4 British economist Angus Maddison's estimate of how much larger GDP per person is now compared with 1820.

What Else?

What if money obeyed the laws of thermodynamics? *See page 22*

What if car production grew as fast as financial trading? *See page 122*

WHAT IF
THERE WERE NO
INTEREST?

Tony Greenham

 The payment of interest by borrowers, and the earning of interest on savings, is commonplace in many cultures. It seems hard to imagine a financial system without interest, but historically, the idea of charging interest has been controversial. Known as usury, the practice was condemned in religious texts from Islam, Buddhism, Judaism, and Christianity. Islamic banking still outlaws interest as usury, although over time in other cultures usury came to mean the charging of excessive interest. Banning interest does not prevent saving and investment. Instead, it requires the investor to share in both the risks and the rewards of the venture being funded. This is known as equity investment: the investor receives a share, or dividend, of profits rather than a fixed payment regardless of the venture's success. If there were no interest, business investment could all be funded in this way and the profits shared between entrepreneurs and investors. Not all borrowing is to fund business ventures, however. In the late 18th century the first building societies emerged in England. Members pooled regular savings and took turns to receive a loan to buy a house. Savings and loans were interest-free and borrowing and lending was a reciprocal arrangement between members. In Scandinavia today the JAK Members Bank makes loans entirely free of interest to its members, who must first make regular savings. In this way, savers and borrowers are always balanced and members cannot keep accumulating debt. JAK's operations are funded by modest administration charges. In a world of interest-free banking, savers would have to alter their expectations. In most banking systems, we expect a return without any risk of loss of money. Indeed, savings are usually guaranteed by the government against the danger of the bank going bust. However, to expect financial return without working or taking any risk is exactly what was meant by usury.

What Then?

Without interest, we would have to choose between storing our savings safely and investing them to earn a return. We might even have to pay fees to store our savings, much like hiring a safety deposit box to store valuable items. On the other hand, if we wanted to earn a return, we would probably be much more concerned than we are now about the people to whom our bank was lending, and what they were going to use our money for.

What Gives?

2,000 percent
Typical equivalent annual interest rate on a short-term "payday" loan.

$1.38 million
Value of $100 after accumulating 10 percent compound interest for 100 years.

What Else?

What if there was no such thing as money? *See page 24*

What if there were no banks? *See page 126*

WHAT IF WOMEN WERE IN CHARGE OF FINANCE?

Ruth Potts

In 2007 two Cambridge University researchers looked at the impact of testosterone on risk and overconfidence in the financial system. They conducted tests on traders to find out if the hormone was higher in winners than losers. Levels were significantly higher on days when traders made more than average profits. If this persisted for several weeks, they speculated, the chronically elevated appetite for risk might have important behavioral consequences. Testosterone has receptors throughout areas of the brain that, neuroeconomics suggests, lead to irrational financial decisions. The researchers suggested women, with 5–10 percent of the circulating testosterone of men, may be less "hormonally reactive." Simply replacing men with women might change the way speculation works, but fails to address stereotypes that created the conditions for the 2007 crash. Finance has been largely deemed to be a "masculine" domain, making it seem as if men are better suited to working in finance, and supposes that only masculine-stereotyped behavior, values, and skills are appropriate. Financiers are assumed to find risk thrilling, be intensely competitive, motivated by self-interest, not to value social relationships, and be technically minded. Due caution in a "macho" culture is dismissed as unnecessary and weak. A more balanced approach is suggested by Norway where a minimum 40 percent quota has been applied to boardrooms. In 2002, women took 6 percent of the seats around Norwegian boardroom tables; six years on it was 44 percent. Norway's approach forces open decision-making, ensuring that more perspectives are heard. It was the only Western industrialized nation to escape the global financial crisis; it has a healthy banking sector and record low unemployment. By adopting Norway's lead, we might develop a more diverse and stable financial system, and also challenge destructive gender stereotypes.

What Then?

If finance valued a wider range of attributes, we could create a more dynamic, responsive system able to adapt to changing circumstances and a myriad of needs. More women in charge of finance might also help break down a wider range of prejudices by challenging stereotypical and often self-reinforcing views of what men and women are good at. Perhaps it might also mean that less money flowed through the speculative financial system.

What Gives?

12 Number of the world's 160 central banks that are headed by women, according to the Central Banking Directory for 2011.

Women campaigners

"Move Your Money" campaigns to encourage consumers to switch money to more ethical banks on both sides of the Atlantic were founded by women: blogger extraordinaire Arianna Huffington in the USA, and campaigner Danielle Paffard in the UK.

What Else?

What if "irrational economic woman" replaced "rational economic man"? *See page 60*

WHAT IF
WE ONLY IMPORTED
THINGS WE COULDN'T
MAKE OR GROW
OURSELVES?

Andrew Simms

 Importing only things we couldn't make or grow ourselves would trigger a large-scale shift in people's skills. Manufacturing, engineering, growing, and processing would experience a renaissance. Apprenticeships in nearly all trades would again become the norm. Reacquainting ourselves with making, growing, and doing, working cloth, wood, or metal would make us more appreciative of all kinds of materials—and other attitudes would alter, too. We would become better at mending things, more averse to waste. Trade would become a smaller share of national income, which would make the economy less vulnerable to shifting currency values and balance of payments. Long-distance freight traffic would reduce greatly and less fuel would be wasted. (If only one country made this change, it would be under extreme pressure from other countries not wishing to do the same, likely resulting in economic "gunboat diplomacy," where some countries tried to force others to take their goods.) A wider range of goods and services would be available domestically. Governments would find it easier to procure from domestic suppliers, which would cause less tax spending to leak out of the country. Added value would come in a higher "multiplier effect" from public spending, that is, money and earnings would circulate more between local producers, making them better off. There might even be a virtuous cycle of job creation and a more resilient economy. The country would still be open for business for those things it could not do for itself. Because imports would be less common, overseas goods would seem more special; this rarity value could lead to a black market developing.

What Next?

It seems likely that there will be growing pressure to import less, as scarcity caused by extreme bad weather leads countries, for example Russia, to suspend grain exports. As a result, national incomes may go down, especially for those involved in trade. Some countries in economic crisis rapidly start adapting with greater self-reliance, but it will be hard for small island nations unable to make all their own produce.

What Gives?

4,836 tons
Amount of yogurt imported to the USA (2004).

4,387 tons
Amount of yogurt exported from the USA (2004).

What Else?

What if we all had to pay for the damage we do to the planet?
See page 102

What if foreign trade was banned?
See page 142

WHAT IF
HOUSES COST THE SAME
AS 30 YEARS AGO?

Tony Greenham

 Whether we buy or rent our home, housing is likely to be the largest expenditure we make during our lives. Many factors can affect the price of houses. As with all markets, the price will reflect demand and supply. A shortage of new houses, or a large increase in population, will drive up house prices. Local factors are also important. If an area becomes more desirable, perhaps because of good schools, new transport links, or other new amenities, its prices will rise relative to neighboring areas. In this case the value of the land has increased because of investments in the area made by businesses and government. In contrast some areas can become so economically depressed that houses become impossible to sell at any price. Unlike many other markets for goods and services, however, houses are purchased mostly with borrowed money. The loans have to be repaid out of the purchasers' incomes. So how easy it is to get a mortgage, how high the interest rate is, and how confident lenders and borrowers both feel about their ability to repay the loan all have a major impact on the prices of houses. Big shifts in confidence and the price and availability of mortgages can lead to housing bubbles and busts that have been observed in many countries. During the Japanese property bubble in 1986–90 the price of properties rose as much as six or seven times. Even after the bubble burst, housing remained very expensive in Japan, where 100-year mortgages are commonplace. Ignoring the booms and busts, in many countries the price of homes has increased over time by more than wages. In the UK the average house costs 4.4 times the average income, whereas in 1983 it was only 2.7 times. Rents also tend to increase with house prices. This means that even though incomes are much higher than 30 years ago, we have to use even more of our income than before to pay for a place to live.

What Then?

If house prices could be reduced to levels seen 30 years ago, the amount of household income spent on mortgage repayments and rent would fall. Living standards would improve as people would have more income to spend on other things or could work fewer hours. However, the factors affecting house prices are complex, and when prices fall quickly it can damage the economy and leave some homeowners with debts they are unable to pay.

What Gives?

637 percent
The increase in average house prices in the UK over the 30 years 1982–2012.

$215,000
Highest price per square meter for prime commercial property in Tokyo in 1989 at the top of the property bubble.

13.5 times
The multiple of house prices to annual income in the world's least affordable city, Hong Kong.

What Else?

What if we let anybody live anywhere? *See page 72*

What if there was no interest? *See page 80*

HISTORICAL
WHAT IF TULIPS
ARE PRICELESS?

There was a time when tulips were the most valuable commodity on Earth, as the result of a collective insanity in the sophisticated markets of the Netherlands in the 1630s. In a few months in 1636, traders managed to push tulip bulbs up to ruinous prices and then watched with horror while the prices collapsed in a few short weeks in February 1637. This was the first of many disastrous bubbles in various markets that have briefly made those involved wealthy, only to ruin them later—the first of a succession of insane explosions that have carried on into our own day.

Tulips only arrived in western Europe in 1554 and they were not widely cultivated in the Dutch Republic until the 1590s. Within a few years, the bulbs for these distinctive flowers became coveted luxury items for the wealthy traders around Amsterdam who were making a fortune out of the Dutch East Indies. The tulips bloomed only for a week in the spring, and the rest of the time the bulbs—especially those of the exotic new colors—were traded on the markets.

The sophisticated financial traders in Amsterdam soon created a futures market in which investors could buy bulbs in the future at the end of the season. The prices rose steadily and began to rise even faster by 1634, once French speculators became involved. Contracts to buy bulbs at the end of the season were bought and sold in taverns in Amsterdam at very high prices. It was known as "wind trade" because nothing actually changed hands except for pieces of paper and, by the late summer of 1636, these were changing hands sometimes at the rate of 10 times a day.

Writing two centuries later, Scottish journalist Charles MacKay, author of *Extraordinary Popular Delusions and the Madness of Crowds*, described how "nobles, citizens, farmers, mechanics, seamen, footmen, maid-servants, even chimney-sweeps and old clotheswomen, dabbled in tulips. People of all grades converted their property into cash, and invested it in flowers. Houses and lands were offered for sale at ruinously low prices, or assigned in payment of bargains made at the tulip-mart. Foreigners became smitten with the same frenzy, and money poured into

Holland from all directions. The prices of the necessities of life rose again by degrees: houses and lands, horses and carriages, and luxuries of every sort rose in value with them, and Holland seemed the very antechamber of Plutus."

Tulip bulbs suddenly reached extraordinary prices, and the rarest were bought for speculation. Some of them reached prices worth 10 times the average manual worker's wage for a year. Strange stories circulated about people who bought them thinking they were onions, ate them by mistake, and found they had consumed the value of a large mansion.

By then the mania had spread to other Dutch cities, and it was in the city of Haarlem that it began to unravel quite suddenly in February 1637, when buyers failed to show up at a regular bulb auction—possibly because there had been an outbreak of bubonic plague. The panic spread, the market for bulbs collapsed, and prices fell to about one-hundredth of what they had been at the height of the frenzy.

Modern scholars have wondered whether the classic accounts were correct, and have tried to explain what happened. A new law issued by the Dutch Parliament in November 1636 seems to have encouraged speculation by redefining the contracts as "options," which meant that people would not actually have to buy the bulbs when the date became due but would have to compensate the seller for a small percentage of the contract—encouraging traders to believe this was a risk-free investment.

WHAT IF
ONE COUNTRY DEFIED
THE MARKETS?

Ruth Potts

 We know a little about what might happen because of what happened when Iceland defied the markets after its financial crisis, which began in 2008. Relative to the size of its economy, Iceland's banking collapse was the largest in economic history. It was the first rich country in more than three decades to be bailed out by the International Monetary Fund. Yet, by 2013, Iceland's economy was set to grow by 2.7 percent, while the British economy teetered on the precipice of triple-dip recession. A budget deficit that had reached 13.5 percent of Icelandic GDP in 2009 fell to 2.3 percent in 2011. Iceland claims that this success was the result of defying the global markets. Iceland let its banks fail (the heads of two of its biggest banks were put on trial) and imposed capital controls, making it harder for foreign investors to take money out of the country. Critics suggest that its economy was vastly inflated, and then destroyed by the nation's crude embrace of free-market policies. But after the crash Iceland rejected those policies as rapidly as it had adopted them. Conventional wisdom suggests that defying the markets can spell disaster for nations, including a collapse of the value of their currency. The case of Iceland suggests that it need not be like that. Certainly the ratings agencies might not like defiance, which could make it impossible to borrow from international markets. We don't know for certain what the impact might be, but it would certainly help if nations defied the markets together. Capital controls would impose costs—it would mean a new bureaucracy to police how much money people sent out of the country and it would be hard to do—but they might also give governments more freedom to create the money they needed without panicking the global traders. Breaking the rules might just pay off and help nations invest for a brighter future.

What Then?

If one country defied the markets, its economy could focus less on financial services and might even begin to serve the needs of the many. Capital controls would allow the nation to plan for the future, rather than tumble unprepared into it. It might even encourage other countries to do the same and fashion a very different global economy where communities, rather than markets, have the last say.

What Gives?

$32 trillion
The amount a former chief economist at McKinsey estimates that wealthy individuals may have in tax havens.

€30–35 billion
The amount expected to be raised from a Financial Transaction Tax adopted by 11 European states.

What Else?

What if the bulls and bears were locked up? *See page 94*

What if the banks crashed again? *See page 130*

WHAT IF WE STOPPED BUYING STUFF?

Ruth Potts

"I shop, therefore I am." This is an aphorism that underpins the modern economy. Crudely put, when we buy more stuff the economy grows, and it is considered a good thing. So what would happen if we all stopped buying stuff? If we all suddenly stopped and government took no action, the results might well be disastrous, of course. The system, which depends on constant growth, would start to run down. The economy as we know it would implode as money stopped circulating. Governments and companies would beg us to buy to keep the economy afloat. Astounding deals would be on offer, and would still be out of reach of the burgeoning unemployed. For those in debt, the need to earn something would be overwhelming, but there would be opportunities provided by the same people who stopped buying—they would need to repair, reimagine, or share what they already owned. So there would be an upside. Making and mending the things we have takes many skilled hands and could potentially create abundant employment. Collaborative consumption is fashionable, but what if we produced collaboratively, too? We could share, borrow, and repair the things we need—and make more, too. A world in which we all held a wider range of practical skills would leave us less at the mercy of disposable goods and built-in obsolescence, and more able to fashion the world around us in satisfying ways. It would mean less anxiety-inducing choices between almost identical products that are likely to be superseded by a new "must-have" model in moments. We might even find that our lives would be richer and more interesting. If we stopped buying music over the Internet, we would have to make more of our own. If we stopped buying from supermarkets, the growing of food could turn our cities into gardens. Perhaps "we make, therefore we are" might suit us all better.

What Then?

A "new materialist" world in which we made things last longer and endlessly reused them would mean a big shift to services that keep things going. It would mean a huge growth in the numbers of plumbers, electricians, builders, carpenters, farmers, and engineers, as much as upholsterers, seamstresses, painters, and potters. Exploring the full life cycle of "stuff" is creative, intelligent, and thoughtful. By buying less, we might just learn to live more.

What Gives?

3,000 Increase since 1982 in number of advertisements seen every day by a typical city-dweller (up from 2,000 to 5,000 a day). This is an estimate by USA-based market research firm Yankelovich.

1884 Year in which the world's oldest working car, a De Dion "steam Runabout," was made. The car, which was sold in October 2011, was looked after by one family for 81 years.

What Else?

What if work was fun?
See page 36

What if we only imported things we couldn't make or grow ourselves?
See page 84

WHAT IF
THE BULLS AND BEARS
WERE LOCKED UP?

David Boyle

 In Wall Street, the financial district of New York City, there is a huge statue of a charging bull, like a mildly idolatrous religion at the heart of the district—a symbol of all the hopes of the financial system: that it should be like a rampaging bull, rather than a shy bear. Imagine we locked them both away and calmed down the markets, and perhaps even locked up the speculators as well. The returns from financial services would certainly go down, although there is evidence to suggest that current speculative flows are not actually very productive—so they might not go down that much. There would also be a large number of unemployed financial managers. Our pensions might suffer, but the financial system would be more secure, and we would be at less risk from the flows of speculative money that dwarf the money doing what money is supposed to do—buying goods and services. Locking up the bulls and bears would mean locking up the people the American business writer Thomas L. Friedman called the "electronic herd," who keep government spending in check by diving in and out of government bonds depending on their risk value. If the speculators were locked up in some small casino somewhere to gamble away to their hearts' content, we might be able to organize a better system for doing what the stock market is supposed to do: help businesses raise the money they need to expand. The bulls and the bears are too wrapped up in their prevailing mood to see these potential investments very clearly. We may not be able to imagine a world without any of their influence, but we might be able to imagine one in which they dominate a bit less.

What Then?

This begs the big question: is it really possible to invent a better system than stock markets, with all those bulls and bears, when it comes to raising money? The answer is probably not, but we could have smaller ones, or regional ones, or specialist or ethical ones—anything where we are in less danger of being trampled to death when the bulls and bears roam too near the doors.

What Gives?

$4 trillion
Amount of money that flows through the world markets every day.

95 percent
Proportion of that amount that is speculation.

What Else?

What if women were in charge of finance? *See page 82*

What if one country defied the markets? *See page 90*

The notional value of

the world derivatives market is

11 times the size of the world economy

$791,000,000,000,000

=

GREEN

INTRODUCTION
GREEN

Economists were confused about the environment for a long time. Classical economics suggests that there were three kinds of capital, the three factors which, combined together, can create wealth: land, labor, and money. But that led to a strange, partial understanding of what was actually going on because it involved turning a blind eye to the absolutely vital role of Nature in the process. Raw materials would emerge as if from nowhere, be turned into products with a price—at which point the economists would notice them—and then be thrown away and, as far as economics was concerned, they might as well have disappeared in a puff of smoke.

One of the side effects of this blindness was that "natural capital"—one of those new kinds of capital that economists have imagined—could be used up, polluted, or poisoned in some way without economists noticing. The feminist economist Marilyn Waring used the example of a forest. While it grew, it had no economic value. There was only an economic value when it was chopped down and turned into toothpicks.

Thanks to the work of ecological and environmental economists over the past generation, these peculiarities are beginning to be ironed out of economics—although it has taken policymakers a long time to catch up. But there are still many ways in which rival economic disciplines try to incorporate the planet into their calculations and models. Sometimes they assign values to the environment, whether it is for elephants or glaciers—or even the Moon—so that they are accounted for properly. Other economists say that these assets are beyond price and they must be accounted for in some other way. There are peculiarities and drawbacks to both methods, and both ways forward lead to other questions.

This section tries to ask some of these, such as what would happen if we all had to pay for the environmental damage in the world—now, rather than later? Or what would happen if we left all the oil in the ground? Or even: what would happen if we all had our very own personal carbon ration? It is time to test your opinion against those of the economists here.

WHAT IF
THE WORLD
STOPPED FLYING?

Andrew Simms

Today flying is taken for granted, at least by those able to afford it. But what if the world stopped flying, or flew far less? There was a glimpse in 2010 of what life without flying might be like. When the Icelandic volcano Eyjafjallajökull erupted, climatic conditions and the nature of the eruption sent a vast cloud of dust lethal to aircraft engines over the flight paths of northern Europe. For days, no aircraft was allowed to fly. Somehow, though, people managed. Businesses used video-conferencing instead of sending staff in person—saving time, money, and carbon emissions. Norway's prime minister, Jens Stoltenberg, stranded in New York, reportedly ran the Norwegian government using his iPad. Travelers took to trains, boats, buses, and shared cars. Social media came into its own, uniting strangers who were heading the same way. Stores turned to local suppliers. Had the grounding of aircraft continued much longer, countries with industries reliant on air freight to export highly perishable goods such as salads or flowers would have had a big problem. Such industries tend to be intensive users of water and energy that return few local economic benefits, so the loss of flights could be a chance to consider more robust economic alternatives. Similarly, regions dependent on long-distance tourism would need to find other livelihoods as tourists took vacations nearer home. Around 2,000 airlines currently make about 28 million scheduled flights each year from 3,700 airports around the world. But rich countries dominate, with 11 million of all flights accounted for by airlines from the USA. This suggests that if the world did stop flying, most of the world's population would not, in fact, be directly inconvenienced. For others, long journeys would become more time-consuming affairs not taken glibly, yet possibly appreciated more.

What Next?

Abandoned airfields could become tourist attractions, like the Mojave Air and Space Port in California. Flying will get more expensive as rising demand for oil meets limited supply, but one estimate for aviation growth takes up the UK's entire national fair share of carbon emissions by the year 2040, so—to avoid global warming—a major reduction may well be essential, which means designing our food, trade, and transport systems to be less reliant on flying.

What Gives?

500,000 Estimated average number of people airborne at any one moment.

380 Number of hours people in the UK spend traveling each year. You might think that faster, modern transport like aviation has saved us travel time. But the UK's National Travel Survey, run since 1972, reveals that people spend about the same time traveling now as they did then.

What Else?

What if we all had to pay for the damage we do to the planet?
See page 102

What if foreign trade was banned?
See page 142

WHAT IF
WE ALL HAD TO PAY FOR
THE DAMAGE WE DO TO
THE PLANET?

Andrew Simms

 If everyone had to pay for damage done to the planet, our food, transport, and homes would be very different. Anything needing a great deal of energy to make or do would be far more costly. We would fly less, relying more on online communication to keep in touch with colleagues, friends, or family. Vacations would be in places easily accessed by public transport, by bike, or on foot. Day-to-day, individual car use would be a costly luxury. We might share or use a car on a short-term lease, but the default position would be traveling on mass transit systems such as trains, streetcars, and buses. Many native, seasonal fruit and vegetables previously allowed to decline would be revived to substitute for the overseas varieties—routinely shipped thousands of miles—that supermarkets trained us to take for granted. This would benefit rural economies and create more jobs in farming and food production. Everybody would be energy-conscious, leading to a burst of activity insulating homes and installing more efficient heating systems. The "standby" culture of having countless electronic gadgets, each with its own high-embodied energy (and therefore pollution), at our beck and call would change. Instead of every home having dozens of such devices—games, phones, TV/computers, and home office kit—many of questionable usefulness, often with built-in obsolescence disguised as regular "upgrades," we would have one or two key multifunctional objects. Anything else would be shared or borrowed when needed from collaborative neighborhood schemes or local gadget-lease hubs. Everything would be made to have a minimum 10-year lifespan, be repairable, and ultimately recyclable. Planet-friendly choices would become the affordable options. Anything wasteful of precious resources would cost.

What Next?

The change in habits driven by actually having to pay the full cost of all the stuff we accumulate would prove hard. Consumerism has been like a fostered addiction and—as always—going "cold turkey" would not be easy. Vested interests in keeping the old way of doing things would campaign hard for maintaining the status quo. There would be considerable resistance, complaints about infringements of liberty, and angry blogs. There would also be highly complex arguments about exactly what should be charged to what.

What Gives?

£6 billion The hidden cost of the aviation industry in the UK according to the European Environment Bureau.

Over $500 billion Annual subsidy to the fossil fuel sector, according to the International Energy Agency.

What Else?

What if the world stopped flying? *See page 100*

What if we all had our own carbon ration? *See page 114*

HISTORICAL
WHAT IF CHARGING
INTEREST IS ILLEGAL?

For most of the first millennium of the Christian Church, doctrine forbade anyone to lend money and charge interest on it. Doing so was like being paid twice for the same thing, said the great Italian theologian Thomas Aquinas. Christians called charging interest "usury," but this did not quite make it illegal.

The first Holy Roman Emperor, Charlemagne, made usury a criminal offence in the 8th century, and for the rest of the medieval period the popes struggled against emerging banks that charged interest despite the teachings of the Church. In 1311 Pope Clement V declared that any laws supporting usury were null and void—since 1179, anyone caught charging interest had been excommunicated from the ministry of the Church.

In the medieval period it was very difficult to get loans—but not impossible. If you wanted to borrow money to go on pilgrimage, for example, the abbeys would lend it to you, for a fee. If you wanted to borrow money to extend your home or fortifications, then you could go to the financial services sector. This was largely the Jewish community, who were excluded from involvement in other work and who were permitted by their own scriptures to charge foreigners interest.

The result was that those providing loans became deeply unpopular. The latest research on the murderous riots against the Jews in England in the 1190s shows that they were instigated by young aristocrats trying to avoid their debts. At the height of the York riots in 1190, the debt documents were burned in a great pyre in the nave of York Minster. One of the strange by-products of making interest illegal was the spread of anti-Semitism.

Italian and German banks began to emerge, like the Medici of Florence or the German Fugger family. These banks did not strictly charge interest, but specified fines for late payments of a noninterest bearing loan or arrangement fees. By the Reformation in the 16th century, the definition of usury in Europe was changed so that it condemned the practice of charging excessive interest, but lending money at interest was allowed. The world changed as a result.

Among Muslims, meanwhile, charging interest had always been condemned on the grounds that growing money as if it were a living thing is unnatural and against God's law. (In Islam the word for usury is *riba*, which literally means "excess" or "addition.") Muslims developed a series of practical alternatives to charging interest, mainly by sharing the risk and rewards between lender and borrower. Over the past generation, Islamic banking has begun to grow as an economic force in its own right, starting in 1975 with the establishment of the Islamic Development Bank. Most big international banks now have an Islamic department and Islamic banking is one of the fastest-growing sectors of the financial services industry.

Islamic banks work differently from Western banks. They do not create money in the form of loans, as Western banks do. In theory, all their loans are backed 100 percent by the money they have on deposit—although that is never quite achieved in practice. This may explain why the Islamic world is less prone to inflation, because charging interest means that loans have to be repaid plus something extra in the future, and prices start to rise.

So there is the answer: if charging interest becomes illegal, you get less inflation and more stable money, but you tend to drive interest underground—or invent systems that avoid it—which can make those involved deeply unpopular. One way or another, people will borrow money and they will pay something to do it.

WHAT IF
EVERY TOWN HAD
ITS OWN CURRENCY?

David Boyle

The mayor of Bristol, UK, recently demanded that his salary be paid in a special city currency that could only be spent locally. If everybody did that—asked to be paid in their own neighborhood "groat" or "token"—trade would certainly become difficult and expensive. What currency should the contract specify? How should the various costs of transport be paid, given that every time travelers crossed the border of another town they would have to change their money? But national currencies have only existed for five centuries or so; before that, medieval traders managed with a mixture of city currencies, some of which they trusted enough to save and some of which they spent as soon as they could. In the USA, until the 1860s, every shopkeeper would keep a huge book known as a "counterfeit detector" next to the cash register, because of the multiplicity of different banknotes issued by every tiny bank in the nation—and beyond. Local currencies are complicated to handle. On the other hand, big single currencies may be useful, but they don't measure everything very well—even within the same nation. Single currencies are geared to suit the needs of the bankers that issue them, but may not suit other countries or cities so well because the interest rates are too high for them to be able to trade—which is why the euro ran into trouble in southern Europe. Not all nations are what they call "optimal currency areas," so there may still be advantages in having a range of currencies—international, national, and local—to choose from every day. If every town had its own currency, the main consequence would be the rapid growth of money changers. However well you managed the multiplicity of different kinds of money you earned, you would still need to do some conversion—and conversion, because it would be risky, would be a lucrative business for the new cadre of money changers.

What Then?

In the long term a world in which everywhere has its own currency would require complex electronic wallets. These would collect and exchange a huge number of currencies simultaneously and help us decide which to spend immediately—and be glad to be rid of—and which to stash away for a rainy day. This would be a complicated business, and quite impossible before computers. But with cell phones as electronic wallets, who knows?

What Gives?

244 Number of different local currencies listed on www.complementarycurrency.org

$4 trillion Amount of money in foreign exchange trading every day between currencies in 2012.

What Else?

What if there was no such thing as money? *See page 24*

What if there were no banks? *See page 126*

WHAT IF
WE COULD BUY ONLY
FAIR TRADE BANANAS?

Tim Leunig

 Bananas are cheap even in countries that do not grow bananas. They are usually cheaper than apples, a bunch of grapes, or pretty much any other fruit. They are also usually cheaper than a candy bar. Fair-trade bananas are slightly more expensive—but only slightly. If we could buy only fair-trade bananas the price of bananas would rise, but most people wouldn't even notice. They would eat the same number of bananas as ever. Someone would be worse off somewhere, however, as people can only spend money once. Spending a little more on bananas means a little bit less money left over at the end of the month. Something, somewhere would have to give. A few people would notice and would eat slightly fewer bananas. They would buy more apples or candy bars. The danger is that if this happened to any significant extent, less money rather than more might end up flowing to the poor countries that grow bananas. The people most likely to notice the rise in price are people in emerging nations, where consumers are that bit poorer, and that bit more price-conscious. Those people would eat fewer bananas. In all probability they would eat more of their staple foods, such as rice. Their diet would be slightly worse as a result. Because bananas are cheap, and the effect on the price is small, most banana growers would gain: the rise in the price they receive would in all likelihood more than compensate for the fall in the number of bananas sold in emerging economies. Not all banana growers would be better off, however. Some would not be able to meet the administrative standards required to prove that they meet the fair-trade standards. Often these would be the poorest farmers, who would be less likely to be literate and able to cope with the necessary bureaucracy.

What Then?

There are dangers for farmers if fair trade becomes too generous. If that happens, banana growing would become very profitable. Then many more people would decide to grow bananas, to try to get a slice of the profits. The supply of bananas would then exceed demand for bananas, many of which would be left unsold. Fair trade does not work if no one wants to buy the product.

What Gives?

1 in 4 Proportion of
bananas sold in the UK that are fair trade.

27.5 million Tons
of cotton produced in the world every year.

11 percent
Fair-trade cotton's share of the total cotton market.

What Else?

What if we only imported things we couldn't make or grow ourselves?
See page 84

What if foreign trade was banned?
See page 142

WHAT IF
THERE WERE ENOUGH
FOOD FOR EVERYONE?

Andrew Simms

If everyone got enough to eat, the results might be surprising. Having large families is often an insurance policy where more children die due to hardship. Secure against hunger, one of the pressures of population growth would diminish. Similarly, less competition for resources might reduce conflict. But is everyone eating enough a realistic expectation? Around 800–900 million people in the world are thought to be undernourished. Yet there is already more than enough food to feed everyone. People go hungry because of inequality, war, and poverty. There is a lack of help from governments—especially to the small-scale farmers, poor and marginalized, who need it most. Bad distribution and growing crops for biofuels and cattle fodder, also explain the persistence of hunger. Everyone could get enough to eat if people had sufficient power and resources—money, seeds, or land—to guarantee access to food, and if support went to the food systems best able to secure the needs of the hungry. A warming world makes it harder to grow crops in some countries. Intensive industrial farming depletes and exhausts the soil, and relies on expensive, polluting fossil fuels to make fertilizers, operate big farm machines, and transport crops for export. In 2008, weather extremes ruined crops and high oil and gas prices pushed up food costs. The United Nations estimated that the additional number of people worldwide who fell into hunger was 75 million. Rising energy costs makes growing crops for biofuels more profitable than food for human consumption. Farming to provide for a meat-based diet demands more energy, water, and land, making it harder to ensure everyone gets enough food. Preventing hunger in the long term means more equal sharing of resources, diets with less meat, and more ecological approaches to farming.

What Next?

Ecological farming techniques only receive a tiny fraction of the money available for research. In spite of that, green methods to improve the soil, reduce erosion, and benefit nutrition can raise farm yields by 60–195 percent, according to the United Nations Food and Agriculture Organization. What all this means is that, even with a growing population and a switch to greener farming methods, everyone could get enough to eat.

What Gives?

800 million Number of people who could be fed by the grain eaten by livestock in the USA, at levels in the 1990s. This calculation was made by David Pimentel, professor of ecology at Cornell University in Ithaca, New York.

120 billion Projected global livestock count in 2050—double the current 60 billion count, according to the United Nations Food and Agriculture Organization.

What Else?

What if we all had to pay for the damage we do to the planet? *See page 102*

What if we all had our own carbon ration? *See page 114*

WHAT IF WELL-BEING WERE THE MAIN PURPOSE OF ECONOMICS?

Andrew Simms

 Conventional economic theory supposes that the more we buy, the better off we are. Yet consuming more stuff is only linked to improvements in human well-being in places where material needs are not already being met. In North America and Europe, economies have been growing for decades with no similar increase in life satisfaction. People who consume very little have an equal chance of happiness as those who shop till they drop. Extensive research with men and women of different ages, backgrounds, cultures, and nationalities has shown that people who place importance on money, image, and status are less likely to be happy than those who are less concerned with these matters. Materialism, it seems, is not very good for you. An economy that made greater human well-being its main purpose would probably seek to maximize five things proven to enhance life satisfaction. One is connecting with people—so, for example, real human contact would replace self-checkouts and automated phone systems. Another is being physically active, so towns would be designed to facilitate walking and cycling. A third is taking notice of the world—being open, attentive, and curious; the proliferation of urban advertising might be checked, to let the real world peep through and make way for public art and other types of creativity. Learning matters, too, suggesting a focus on more trade apprenticeships and commitment to lifelong education. We feel better for giving, so we might make it the norm to give our time to schools and health services and share with friends and neighbors to meet our travel needs. Sharing schemes for everything, from cars to tools and a range of skills, are increasingly popular, and people now talk about "collaborative consumption."

What Next?

Increasingly governments are collecting data to show if our well-being is going up, or down. The next step is to use this information to judge whether different policies raise or lower well-being. That might lead to some bolder initiatives, like shifting to a shorter working week. This could be copied by other countries who saw the benefits, or exploited by those still prioritizing mainly money as wealth.

What Gives?

Costa Rica Best
country on Earth? Costa Rica came top in the Happy Planet Index in 2012. The index measures how resource-efficient a nation is at creating relatively happy, long lives that don't wreck the environment.

Norway Highest ranked
Western European country in the Happy Planet Index in 2012—in 29th place.

105 The USA's ranking in the
Happy Planet Index 2012, out of 151 countries on the index.

What Else?

What if the working week was three days long? *See page 38*

WHAT IF WE ALL HAD OUR OWN CARBON RATION?

Andrew Simms

You get up in the morning and have to make a choice: will you fly to Mexico for a vacation or keep your car on the road for the next month? You can't have both because carbon rationing has been introduced: society no longer rations what you consume by price alone, but by the impact your consumption has on life-supporting ecosystems. It sounds tough, but there could be some benefits. Rich people typically have higher emissions, the result of bigger houses, larger and more cars, and overseas vacations. Because of that, a consequence of a policy to prevent climate change would be that the social pressure that fuels competitive and conspicuous consumption would be reduced. Similarly, a more equal society would bring a range of benefits, from better health and education to reduced crime. Narrowing choices on the basis of whether or not they are carbon-intensive might make it easier to choose what to do, which is good for well-being. Often, if not always, a lower-carbon choice means that more local goods, services, and entertainment become attractive options. This would restore life to our towns and main streets. Organic food that took less fossil fuel to produce would become relatively cheaper, as would diets with less meat in them. Investors would switch from oil, coal, and gas to renewable energy technologies. Public transport would be cheaper and traveling by train, streetcar, bus, and bicycle would be a far better deal. With emissions reduced, air quality would rise dramatically— improving the nation's health and well-being, for example, reducing childhood asthma. There was a time when we thought it was a good idea to guess the demand for new cars and then build the roads for them. In official circles it was called "predict and provide." Carbon rationing balances how to meet everyone's needs with the inescapable tolerance limits of the biosphere.

What Next?

The introduction of carbon rationing would lower conventional economic growth. In turn, this would raise fears of unemployment and cast doubt on our capacity to pay for health, education, and retirement. More job-intensive "green collar" sectors would have to compensate. Although greater equality would lower social bills, in schools, the health system, and care sectors a new model of reciprocity would be needed—with everyone playing some role—to reduce costs and pressure on services, and increase effectiveness.

What Gives?

Norfolk Island, in the Pacific Scene of the world's first experiment in carbon rationing.

$5.5 billion
Value of carbon permits traded around the world in 2006.

$705 million
Value of carbon "offsets" bought voluntarily around the world to compensate for carbon burned, particularly by flying, in 2008.

What Else?

What if we all had to pay for the damage we do to the planet?
See page 102

WHAT IF
WE LEFT THE OIL AND
COAL IN THE GROUND?

Andrew Simms

 Oil has been called "black gold," and coal "bottled sunshine." Some talk of the dawn of a new golden age for the fossil fuel industry in the early 21st century because new technology allows gas and oil that was once inaccessible—trapped in hard-to-mine rock formations such as shale and tar sands—to be extracted. But what if we left it in the ground? In 2009 a study led by German scientist Malte Meinshausen from the Potsdam Institute in Germany quantified how much of remaining fossil fuels we can safely burn. Use too much and the odds shift toward warming the climate to a level at which climate change feeds off itself in an increasingly uncontrollable spiral. To have a good chance of preventing that happening, we can afford to burn only about a fifth of proven fossil fuel reserves. For a world increasingly addicted to fossil fuel use it would be a great shock to reduce consumption by so much and so fast. Would the shock be too much to bear? For most of the things we rely on fossil fuels to do, there are alternatives. We would have to follow a plan like the one by American scientists Mark Jacobson and Mark Delucchi, who devised a global scheme to provide 100 percent of humanity's energy needs from clean, renewable sources such as wind, water, and solar energy technologies. In their version, the shift would take about 20 years, and would use a mix of 3.8 million large wind turbines (wind being 25 times more carbon-efficient than nuclear power), 90,000 solar plants and a combination of geothermal, tidal, and rooftop solar-photovoltaic installations. The plan avoids nuclear power (which requires nonrenewable fuel sources) and coal plants with carbon capture and storage (because that technology is unproven at scale). Some things would change more, however. Biofuels could sustain nothing like the world's current aviation industry, so people would have to fly less.

What Then?

The way we grow food, travel, and generate electricity would all be different. We would have more organic food, and less grown with synthetic chemicals. There would be more electric-powered transport and mass transit such as streetcars and trains. More things would be made nearer to where they are bought and consumed. Disposability would go in favor of things made to last and be cherished.

What Gives?

Just over a day
Amount of time in which an American generates the same amount of carbon emissions produced by someone in Tanzania over a whole year. From the stroke of New Year, the American would generate that level of emissions by early morning on January 2, while a British person would do so by the evening of January 4.

22 billion Number
of human slaves required to produce the energy needed to replace fossil fuels in the world economy, working round the clock, according to "peak oil" theorist Colin Campbell.

What Else?

What if the world stopped flying?
See page 100

FINANCE

INTRODUCTION
FINANCE

I n his *General Theory of Employment, Interest and Money* the great British economist John Maynard Keynes wrote that, "speculators may do no harm as bubbles on a steady stream of enterprise. But the position is serious when enterprise becomes the bubble on a whirlpool of speculation. When the capital development of a country becomes a by-product of the activities of a casino, the job is likely to be ill-done."

Keynes was writing in 1936, only seven years after the Wall Street Crash in 1929 that ushered in the Great Depression—and took Keynes himself by surprise (he was a successful speculator). In the three-quarters of a century since he was writing, the weight of speculation has long since dwarfed the real economy of goods and services, and finance has become a world of its own, little understood outside its own sphere. The huge rewards that emerged for those who were most deeply involved have made finance the dominant element of the global economy, one that draws from a range of other disciplines outside economics, including psychology, physics, and advanced mathematics.

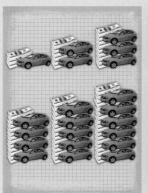  

The modern world of finance is a strange new creation. For those who think that the old-fashioned bank managers are still at their desks, deciding about loan requests personally, or that the financial system is still doing what it used to do—primarily allocating capital to the most productive places—then it is a bit of a shock to discover that there are computers in warehouses across the USA that are trading shares at the rate of 10,000 a second.

Henry Ford used to say that it was a good thing that most people could not understand the way that the financial system worked, because "if they did, I believe there would be a revolution before tomorrow morning." But this implies that questions are not such a good idea, that the status quo is so fragile that a few queries about what might happen would be enough to bring finance crumbling down. This chapter takes the risk of asking some pertinent "what if" questions anyway: what if all money was linked to gold in the way that it used to be? What if we abolished banks altogether? What if car manufacturing grew as fast as financial trading? These are all important questions, and the answers may be surprising.

WHAT IF
CAR PRODUCTION GREW AS FAST AS FINANCIAL TRADING?

Tony Greenham

Global production of cars increased by 55 percent in the 15 years to 2010. In the same period, energy consumption increased 40 percent and global income by over 50 percent. However, these growth rates pale in comparison with the expansion of global financial trading since 1995. Annual turnover on foreign exchange markets has increased by more than 3.3 times, and the notional value of derivatives contracts, a type of financial instrument, is up by a factor of 30+ to $464 trillion. The amount of credit default swaps, a type of financial derivative, leaped from zero in 2000 to over $62 trillion in 2007. Relative to the value of the trades, it takes very little energy and few materials to buy and sell financial instruments. Digital technology has also expanded the number of products that are services we can enjoy. These appear to be "weightless." Listening to music no longer requires the printing of vinyl, and a trip to a theater, gallery, or masseur is more about consuming an experience than material goods. In theory the economy should be able to grow using relatively fewer natural resources. Some economists question the extent to which this is possible, however, because experiences do use up energy and materials—and the more efficient we become at using resources, the more we consume. Others ask whether financial trading can be completely disconnected from the physical world. English economist Frederick Soddy gave an example comparing two pig farmers. One has two real pigs requiring food, shelter, and disposal of their waste. His herd has natural limits on its ability to grow. The second farmer has two "virtual pigs" that are without physical existence and capable of multiplying without limit. Soddy argued that the value of virtual pigs would eventually collapse relative to real ones, because you cannot eat virtual pigs.

What Then?

If car production had kept pace with the growth in foreign exchange trading, more than 165 million cars would be produced every year. If it had tracked in the growth in the value of the derivatives market, 1.5 billion new cars would be made each year. Of course, unlike trading in financial instruments, production of physical goods can only grow as fast as technology and natural resources allow.

What Gives?

80 million Total number of cars produced in 2011.

$18.2 trillion Value of world exports in 2011.

$2,226.5 trillion Combined annual turnover in foreign exchange and over-the-counter derivatives (2011).

What Else?

What if there were no banks?
See page 126

What if the banks crashed again?
See page 130

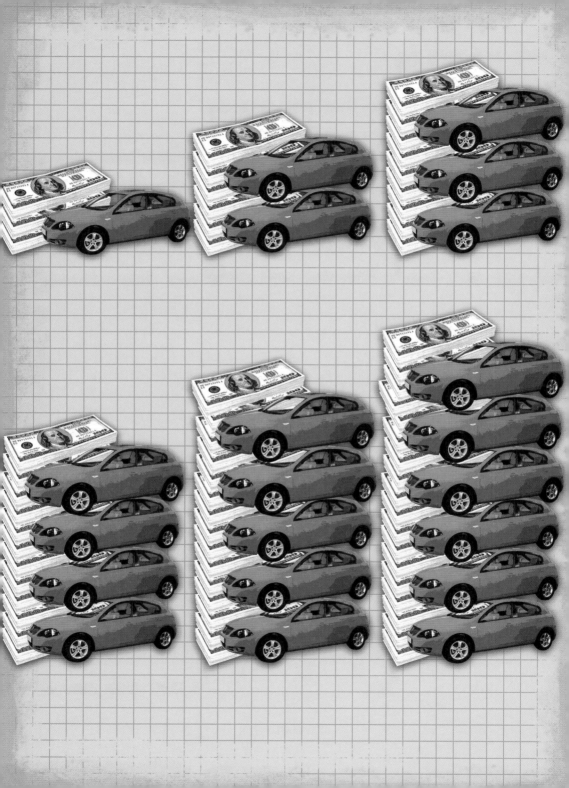

WHAT IF MONEY NEEDED A PASSPORT TO CROSS BORDERS?

Andrew Simms

 Since the easing of controls on the movement of capital in 1979, and after an additional wave of deregulation in the 1990s, so-called "market corrections" look increasingly like ever-larger highway pileups. Each financial crisis seems worse than the last. But what if, when money crossed borders, it was subject to similar checks and balances as people are? It would mean, in effect, making money carry a passport, with terms and conditions applied to its stay in a country. As with people, it would mean knowing what the money intends to do there, how long it will stay, and what it intends to bring in and take out. Capital controls are what prevent the movement of money being a free-for-all. In countries such as Chile, South Korea, and Malaysia, capital controls have been used during crises to insulate against worse economic damage, so we have an idea of what happens: speculation is discouraged and the banks' role changes significantly. If such controls were introduced in, say, New York, a more balanced economy might emerge and the "heat" be taken out of the housing market. The price of homes, long distorted by the bonuses and cash-buying power of executive financial speculators, might become reasonable. Those on lower pay, whose work was nevertheless key to city life—cleaners, nurses, shopworkers—would be able to afford to live nearer their workplace. The "judgment of the markets" (a relatively small number of big financial speculators) would be less feared by policy makers. The habit of high-risk investing (which yielded high returns or bubbles and crashes) would shift. Investors would seek more modest yet reliable returns over the long term, making it more attractive to invest in things such as wind farms and energy-efficient homes.

What Next?

Some sectors of the economy that relied on the booming excesses of footloose capital would be hit hard. Many restaurants and branches of the hospitality industry near financial sectors might close for business. Profits among real estate brokers would fall, and the market for super cars and luxury yachts would take a hammering. A small network of rogue finance states might continue to allow money to flow invisibly from one to another and their continued existence would become deeply controversial as a threat to the new status quo.

What Gives?

20 percent Reserve requirement that must be deposited at the Chilean central bank, redeemable if investments stay put for a year.

$8 billion The amount of "hot money" that left the Turkish economy immediately after their central bank dropped interest rates in 2011.

What Else?

What if we started a world currency? *See page 30*

What if one country defied the markets? *See page 80*

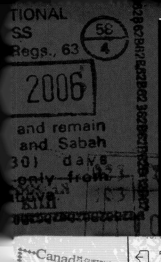

WHAT IF
THERE WERE
NO BANKS?

Tony Greenham

Banks play a central role in modern economies. They operate the mechanisms— electronic bank transfers, credit cards, checks, and ATMs—to allow us to conduct our transactions securely and conveniently. They establish ways for us to invest savings and provide loans to fund business activities, home-buying, and personal consumption. Banks also expand and contract the total amount of money in the economy according to how much new credit they create through a process known as "fractional reserve banking." It has been efficient for banks to carry out these functions for several reasons. They gather information on and develop expertise in choosing the best investments more effectively than we could individually. By pooling our savings, banks reduce the risk for each individual of losing a significant sum. So if there were no banks, we would have to find other ways of carrying out all these activities. Is this possible? New technology has created new ways of making payments. For example, in Kenya the M-Pesa service enables people to make payments using SMS technology and to store money in their cell phone account. Timebanks, local exchange trading schemes, and barter exchanges also allow people to trade without using bank payments, although such schemes are generally seen as complementary to banks, rather than a replacement. Peer-to-peer (P2P) lenders, allow individuals to lend directly to borrowers without using a bank. However, even P2P lenders assess the ability of potential borrowers to repay before letting them join, and they enable savers to pool savings to spread their risk, a little like banks do. Finally, there are alternative systems for creating new money without fractional reserve banking, by the government or central bank issuing money directly into the economy. So theoretically we could manage without banks, but only by finding new ways of doing banking.

What Then?

One of the lessons of regulating money and banks is that people often discover new ways of exchanging, saving, and investing to avoid regulation. In recent years a huge unofficial banking industry has emerged, known as shadow banking. All sorts of institutions from investment funds to energy companies have increasingly engaged in similar activities to banks. So although new technology might one day make today's banks obsolete, the functions of banking are likely to remain.

What Gives?

1472 Founding year of Monte dei Paschi di Siena, the oldest bank still in existence.

$101.6 trillion
Total banking assets of the world's 1,000 largest banks.

$60 trillion Estimated size of the global shadow banking industry.

What Else?

What if there was no such thing as money? *See page 24*

What if every town had its own currency? *See page 106*

HISTORICAL
WHAT IF ALL MONEY IS
BASED ON GOLD?

When Dorothy's dog unmasks the Wizard as a fraud at the end of *The Wonderful Wizard of Oz*, the Scarecrow says to the Wizard: "Really, you ought to be ashamed of yourself for being such a humbug." This was a coded diatribe against basing money on gold—the book's author Frank Baum meant to attack central bankers and their obsession with gold. (Oz is a measure of gold, after all!)

The Wonderful Wizard of Oz was first published in 1900. In those days, and right up to World War I, most money in the world was based on gold. The world's currencies were pegged together on fixed values of gold, and gold bars in the vaults of the biggest central banks—in New York City and London—would be shuffled between cages, representing the different national gold deposits, to balance the books.

It was a world of certainty, with low inflation, when every banknote carried a promise to "pay the bearer on demand" in gold or silver. But it had its drawbacks. It was extremely inflexible and it meant that it favored the people who lent money over the people who borrowed money.

Most nations came off the "gold standard" during World War I because they needed to borrow or create more money than their gold reserves allowed. But when they tried to go back to that world, the attempt proved more difficult than expected. When he put the pound back on the gold standard in 1925, British Chancellor of the Exchequer Winston Churchill painted a romantic picture of international currencies that "vary together, like ships in harbor whose gangways are joined and who rise and fall together with the tide." It was a disaster. British ministers had such an inflated idea of their own value—and that of their nation—that they fixed the pound's value far too high. It meant that British goods became too expensive and factories closed.

A run on the pound in 1931 forced the British pound off the gold standard. (The US dollar stayed on, theoretically at least, until 1971). But immediately, the central bankers began to yearn for the old certainties again, especially the Governor of the Bank of England, Montagu Norman. The great Swiss psychologist Carl Jung, who treated Norman, believed that he was probably insane. It was said that Norman crossed the Atlantic in disguise as a "Mr. Skinner" in 1929, for a secret meeting with US monetary officials and to introduce a short monetary shock intended to force the USA back on the gold standard. Instead, it produced the Great Depression.

The link with gold has been even more bitterly debated in the USA, where the great "bimetallism debate"—over whether to base money on gold, or more plentiful silver—dominated political argument in the final decades of the 19th century. It was then that the American orator William Jennings Bryan made a celebrated speech about gold at the 1896 Democratic Convention. Bryan brought his acceptance speech to a crescendo by raising his arms above his head and then slowly down into the shape of a cross, with the words: "You shall not press down upon the brow of labor this crown of thorns, you shall not crucify mankind upon a cross of gold."

A return to the gold standard seems unlikely these days, but we can see what would happen. It would mean less inflation, but more poverty. It would also mean pretending that all money is basically the same. It would mean effectively that the whole world shared one giant currency.

In the 1990s, bankers dreamed of giant global currencies—Latin American countries enthusiastically linked their currencies to the US dollar, and the European nations pooled their currencies into the euro. When the Argentine peso collapsed as a result, they thought again. Linking the peso to the US dollar gave them stability, but it was a stability that impoverished them—because the dollar was geared to a very different economy. And there is the problem with linking money to gold: it tends to favor the rich and impoverish the poor.

WHAT IF
THE BANKS
CRASHED AGAIN?

David Boyle

 A quick look at history shows that bank crashes have been pretty regular, and seem to be getting more common. The 18th century saw 11 systematic bank crashes, the 19th century had 19, and the 20th century accelerated to 33. Some of these involved only a few banks, but all of them threatened the banking system as a whole. The worst year for bank failures in the USA was 1930, when nearly 1,400 banks closed their doors, but the next worst was 1989. Most of these crashes led to regulation. The US Federal Reserve was the response to the 1907 banking crisis that followed the collapse of the National Bank of North America. The Glass-Steagall Act followed the Wall Street Crash of 1929 and the subsequent banking failures. Yet still they crash. There are three reasons why this gets more dangerous all the time. The first is the speed of the exchanges—shares are traded at the rate of over 10,000 a second by some computers. The second is that nearly $800 trillion in derivative products (the value of which derive from the performance of some other commodity) have now been issued, with untold consequences if they were to unravel, because it is not clear who pays or how much. The third is that the economy is so much more interdependent and brittle than before. The vast majority of supermarkets operate on a just-in-time delivery system. They have no reserves and even a small collapse, whether it is in fuel or credit, can lead to a food shortage. If the financial markets were to collapse again, it could lead rapidly to fuel, food, and energy shortages, unless the authorities were prepared to step in and take action—as they did in 2008—to keep the world's economies functioning. If the financial markets are doing a good job raising money and allocating resources, then it makes sense that they should be better regulated. If they are not, maybe we could imagine something safer and more effective?

What Then?

If we survived the human catastrophe that would follow a general banking collapse, one of the first tasks would be to start new banks. First to open would be local churches, as they did in the Middle Ages, followed by big companies with databases—starting with telephone companies, search engines, and social media websites. Then, as if by magic—there would be banks again, but perhaps more focused than before on what was most important to customers.

What Gives?

98 millionths
of a second The
record speed for a share trade.

$308 billion
Amount in assets of the biggest bank failure ever—Washington Mutual, in 2008.

What Else?

What if the bulls and bears were locked up? *See page 94*

What if there were no banks? *See page 126*

WHAT IF WE REALLY THOUGHT AHEAD?

Helen Kersley

 People care more about today than a year ahead, let alone 50 years' time. Potential short-term gains generally trump long-term ones. We know the importance of the future but struggle to reflect it in decisions (we often underinvest in pension arrangements), business activity (lenders may charge high interest rates on long-term loans), and politics (we postpone action on climate change). This is partly rational, because the future is uncertain, but also irrational, because we know that today's choices affect the future—think of depleting natural resources or making cuts to children's services. Applying economics to policy-making and business decisions formalizes our short-term bias. Cost-benefit analysis helps work out whether the benefits of an investment outweigh its cost. Over and above adjusting for inflation, the rules say you must discount (adjust down) future years' costs and benefits. So, $100 spent or received in 10 years' time might typically count as just $70 in our calculations today. By valuing near-term outcomes more highly we are less likely to invest in projects with longer-term payback. We might also drastically underestimate future costs—for example, pension liabilities—storing up trouble for later. What if we prioritized the future instead? We would care more about long-term outcomes. Investment decisions would favor projects with future benefits over quick wins. As well as seeking longer-term value, we might be more cautious about imposing high risks and costs for future generations. This should build in a bias for sustainability—we would be more likely to use resources sparingly. More profit could be reinvested back into businesses rather than taken as dividends for shareholders, helping to build for future jobs and prosperity. We might seek to invest as much as possible in children, and tackle more vigorously the harms today that will compromise their well-being in adult life.

What Then?

Putting the future first would mean taking actions today to deliver benefits down the line. It would mean paying more attention to intergenerational priorities. But could it simply reverse today's problem and lead to a bias toward the long term, to the detriment of beneficial outcomes today? Luckily that would be largely self-defeating, since poor outcomes today have long-term consequences that our future-first perspective should seek to avoid.

What Gives?

About 50 percent
Proportion of the world's population who won't have enough water by 2030 if we continue on a path of business-as-usual.

£4.7 trillion
The UK government's current unfunded pension liabilities to be paid by future generations.

What Else?

What if there was no interest?
See page 80

What if there was no insurance?
See page 140

BUSINESS

INTRODUCTION
BUSINESS

Economists have always had a divided attitude toward business. On the one hand, business is the practical application of economics—the honeybee that makes the whole business of economic fertilization and circulation possible. On the other hand, business people seem too practical, too compromising, too nitty-gritty compared to the beautiful theorem or economic model to which they are committed.

Yet economics can be a useful discipline for business people, and has proved so ever since Italian mathematician and Franciscan friar Luca Pacioli invented double-entry bookkeeping during the Renaissance. Pacioli's system meant that, at last, medieval merchants had a practical way of working out the value of their cargoes while they were on the high seas—even if it took a year to bring them into harbor.

What has emerged in recent decades is a discipline called "business economics," which tries to apply economic theory and statistics to find ways of analyzing businesses, the way they are organized, and the relationship with employees, customers, and markets. Business economists

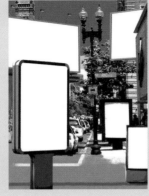

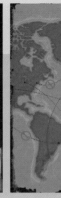

try to explain why companies emerge and why they expand. They try to understand the way entrepreneurs work and how they interact with governments.

Above all, economists can help businesses work out what the likely effect of different changes—especially the big ones—are going to be on their cashflow and profitability, and some of the biggest questions are set out here. What would happen if banned foreign trade? Or what would happen if everyone suddenly stopped shopping in downtown areas (as in many places they already seem to be doing)? Or what would follow if we broke up all the biggest companies into competing units, as the American regulators managed to do so dramatically under President "Teddy" Roosevelt a century ago?

But some of our questions are more human, and they require a different kind of answer. What if women were put in charge of finance? What if human beings simply stopped inventing things? These kind of issues call for the wisdom of a historian or the insights of a psychologist—but they also need the specialist eye of an economist, and that is what we have here.

WHAT IF WE BANNED ADVERTS?

Helen Kersley

 If there were no adverts one of the first things we would notice is space—on streets as billboards became redundant, throughout the media, in sports venues, on trains and buses, and on our doormats. How much would we miss commercial advertising? We might miss some of the artwork and witty slogans. We might not miss the constant marketing pitches and junk mail. But what about the information put out through adverts? How useful is it to us in making choices and learning about new products? Or do we feel bombarded by unwanted information? The role of advertising has always been controversial. Economists have been divided on whether advertising provides valuable information to help consumers make efficient choices or does no more than manipulate people through selective use of information, creating insatiable wants that wouldn't otherwise exist. In 1958 Canadian economist J. K. Galbraith wrote in his book *The Affluent Society* that companies, rather than producing goods to meet people's needs, proactively created the desire for their products. Advertising has also been implicated in fueling a host of ills, from anxiety and dissatisfaction to eating disorders and indebtedness. But counterarguments contend that these problems are not created by advertising but by much deeper systemic forces and pressures in society. Advertising is without doubt a central tool of our economy and market, so banning it would alter the rules of the game. Its absence might slow down the juggernaut of consumption, but that would have an impact on jobs and livelihoods, too—at least until the system adjusted. Many activities and jobs that make up the advertising industry, and others, rely on revenues from it. Would print, broadcast, and online media, for example, find other forms of financing? Would new industries grow up offering alternative jobs for those employed by the ad agencies?

What Then?

If we banned advertising we might expect prices to fall as companies no longer paid for costly advertising campaigns. Yet in competitive markets companies would inevitably seek other methods of marketing to stimulate appetites and encourage consumers to switch to their brand—and these might be equally expensive. The alternatives might be less "noisy" and invasive, however, and we would have the luxury of thinking about what to do with all that space.

What Gives?

$450 billion Global advertising expenditure (estimate) in 2012.

$7.20 Profit for every $1 spent—the benefits to Kentucky Fried Chicken of its new advertising campaign, 2005.

What Else?

What if there was no such thing as money? *See page 24*

What if we stopped buying stuff? *See page 92*

WHAT IF THERE WERE NO INSURANCE?

Tim Leunig

 If there was no insurance people would make more effort to prevent things going wrong. For example, everyone can reduce the risk of being burgled by buying locks and alarms. Similarly, people would build houses on hills to reduce the risk of flooding, or at least demand a large discount before buying a house at the bottom of the valley. You can insure against losing your job by having more than one job. You can work part-time in a store, and be a cab driver for the other half of the week. People would also try to save more, because savings are the classic way of "self-insuring." If you have money in the bank, it isn't the end of the world if someone without insurance crashes into your car and drives off. Savings can also replace health insurance, since you can pay for any treatment you need. Being married is even more attractive in a world without insurance, as you have someone to look after you if things go wrong. Marriage is, in many ways, a mutual lifetime insurance contract, in which the insurance premium is looking after your spouse as necessary, and the return is that he or she will look after you. The most obvious case is being looked after when you are ill, but being married offers many more insurance benefits. For example, if you lose your job, you can live off your spouse's income, or at the very least you can both look for work. Children are the classic long-term insurance policy against being destitute in old age. You need to have several. Some may die before you do. Others may marry and move away. Some may be capricious or simply not like you. Still more may end destitute themselves. It is hard to have too many children in a world without insurance against old age.

What Then?

Insurance is so useful that if it didn't exist we would have to invent it. Commercial insurance markets first began in the medieval era, when people would offer up a piece of land or some such in exchange for an income for life. Markets are good at covering easy-to-define risks—such as your house being burgled or life insurance for an individual. Governments usually cover catastrophic risks, like everyone living longer than expected, or hurricanes hitting a huge area.

What Gives?

6.9 Percentage of world Gross Domestic Product (GDP) spent on insurance.

$5 Spending on insurance per head of population in Bangladesh (2012).

$6,000 Spending on insurance per head of population in the Netherlands (2012).

What Else?

What if there was such a thing as society? *See page 62*

What if houses cost the same as 30 years ago? *See page 86*

WHAT IF FOREIGN TRADE WERE BANNED?

Tim Leunig

 Banning foreign trade would not make that much difference to large countries. Sure, people in the USA would not be able to eat bananas, buy cheap Chinese products, or drive Porsches, but life would go on. Pretty much everything people in the United States want to consume they can make themselves. Indeed, if Porsche were banned from exporting cars to the USA, they might well open a plant there. Because Porsche sell more cars in the USA than in Germany, the USA might well be the only market large enough to support a Porsche plant. Bizarrely, ending foreign trade might make the USA the only place in which Porsches are made and sold. People living in medium-sized countries, however, would find life a lot more boring and more expensive. They would not have the same variety of goods available as now, and prices would be higher. China is very good at producing standardized goods very cheaply—replacing Chinese-made T-shirts with domestically produced T-shirts would definitely involve price rises. And in Norway, say, the cost of growing bananas locally would make them a rare and expensive delicacy, rather than an everyday staple. Ending trade would be really tough for countries without oil or other fuels, who would struggle to remain developed industrial nations. Banning foreign trade would be lethal for very small countries. The world's minnows—tiny places like the Vatican City, or mountainous Andorra—would not be able to feed themselves. Their populations would flee or die. It would also be tragic for developing countries like China. China's development is based on producing cheap manufactured goods and selling them abroad. So an end to foreign trade would mean an end to China's dream of becoming a developed economy. Ending foreign trade would also shut the door on the development dreams of countries like India and Bangladesh, which hope to follow in China's footsteps.

What Then?

Trade almost dried up in the 1930s, and the world became poorer as a result. All of post-1945 economic history has been about supporting international trade. If that was impossible, countries would merge. Small countries would have to—the Vatican City would become part of Italy again, and Andorra would have to choose between France and Spain. European countries (even Britain) would probably merge into a single European super state, and we would see similar "continent countries" elsewhere.

What Gives?

456 Trade as a percentage of Gross Domestic Product (GDP) for Singapore.

25 Trade as a percentage of GDP for the USA.

1.5 Trade as a percentage of GDP for Burma.

What Else?

What if we started a world currency? *See page 30*

What if money needed a passport to cross borders? *See page 124*

WHAT IF WE BROKE UP ALL THE BIG COMPANIES?

Andrew Simms

 If we broke up the big corporations, it would probably become easier to tell where you were in a country. Towns would become noticeably different. Banks, businesses, and stores would vary more from place to place, making local and regional character more distinctive. Imagine also that—as part of these changes—we introduced a new rule under which no company could control more than 5 percent of a given market. There would be much more real choice on offer. Smaller businesses would mean less centralized logistics and outsourcing. This would make it easier for people to put a real face to a product or service—and reduce the hours of frustration that result from being kept at arm's length by a call center or corporate website. It would also mean a more regionally balanced economy. The new kind of market economy would in one sense be less distant and more accountable. But on the other hand, regulators would need to be more vigilant to ensure that workers' rights and public health and safety were respected. The disappearance of dominant blue-chip companies would localize the world of investment. The proportion of the economy locked into the shareholder model and dominated by big finance would shrink. New kinds of pension would emerge that would allow people to invest savings in their local and regional economies, and in local green infrastructure, so that they could benefit from the results of pension investments before retirement as well as after. Because, dollar-for-dollar of turnover, smaller businesses employ more people, jobs would be created. The kind of huge pay ratios that emerge in giant corporations would be impossible to maintain or justify in smaller companies, so the trend toward ever-wider pay ratios would reverse, leading to more general equality.

What Next?

Whether you believe the world would be better depends on whether you think there would be economies or diseconomies of scale. Opponents of the idea would argue that smaller organizations would be less efficient and less innovative, although most evidence suggests that innovation tends to emerge from small companies. The challenge is designing regulation to keep markets open and prevent the irony of supposedly free markets creating monopolies and oligopolies.

What Gives?

30 Number of big food retailers who, between them, now account for one-third of global grocery sales.

90 percent Proportion of the world grain trade now controlled by five companies.

What Else?

What if the bulls and bears were locked up? *See page 94*

What if we relied on the private sector to enforce contracts? *See page 150*

WHAT IF EVERYONE STOPPED SHOPPING ON MAIN STREET?

Andrew Simms

 If we all stopped shopping on main street, it would probably be because of this—or a similar—chain of events: independent food stores closed due to competition from supermarkets; bank branches closed because they didn't make enough profit; cuts closed post offices; shop rents only ever went up, making it tougher for small, local businesses; more people shopped online; finally, even pharmacies—often the last bastions of local shopping—fell prey to deregulation that allowed big retailers to capture the market. Without people shopping on the streets, there would be fewer folk about to bring towns alive. They would become desolate places—boarded-up and litter-strewn. Local spending power that might have created jobs and let downtown areas prosper would leak away, eroding the local tax base. A spiral of decline would set in, especially as graffiti and broken windows began to appear, for most properties are owned by remote landlords, property companies, chains, and, ultimately, hedge funds. Too few people would live locally to care or take responsibility. Self-reinforcing patterns of antisocial behavior and rising crime would drive even more people away. With fewer people meeting casually on the street, surrounding communities would be less friendly and lonelier places. Fewer people would join clubs and societies and, feeling disengaged, would be less likely to go to local events or volunteer in the community. Neighbors would withdraw into their own homes and shop even more online, or drive to out-of-town retail parks. General levels of anxiety and alienation might rise, mutual trust might fall. It would become apparent that a vibrant main street had been the invisible social and economic glue that held communities together, and without it a hard-to-reverse decay would set in.

What Next?

As people felt less and less connected to their community, their sense of well-being and engagement might decline. Voter turn out would go down, as research has shown it did in these circumstances in the USA. Rising levels of depression would manifest in a range of health problems, putting greater pressure on health services. Seeing the consequences of dying main streets, incentives might be introduced to encourage local businesses to open in empty premises. There might be a fightback based on lower local taxation and lower rents.

What Gives?

276 Average number of retail jobs lost in a 10-mile (16-km) radius when a new out-of-town superstore opens (UK).

$11.4 billion Estimates in lost local sales tax every year in the USA because products are bought online.

19 percent Vacancy rates in neighborhood stores in the USA in 2012.

What Else?

What if we broke up all the big companies? *See page 144*

HISTORICAL
WHAT IF WE FINE COUNTRIES
WHEN THEY MISBEHAVE?

As a young man, the great British economist John Maynard Keynes went to Paris to advise his country's prime minister, David Lloyd George, at the peace negotiations to end World War I. The result was the Treaty of Versailles, which imposed such huge fines—or reparations—on Germany that it ruined the economy of the world.

Keynes arrived for the negotiations at the beginning of 1919 with the other national delegations, hoping that President Woodrow Wilson's high-minded approach would restrain the British and French from damaging Germany too much. As time went on, and Keynes's health got worse, he became increasingly infuriated by Wilson's failure and by the bellicose demands of Lloyd George and the French president, Georges Clemenceau, until finally he went home in despair and began writing the book that would make his name.

He wrote pen portraits of the national leaders, condemning Wilson for refusing to forgive American war loans, which also threatened to suck money out of Europe for another generation. These portraits made people laugh, which is always unusual in a book about economics. As a result, *The Economic Consequences of the Peace* was an immediate bestseller on both sides of the Atlantic, confirming to the Americans that they were right not to support the treaty—and right not to endorse Wilson's new League of Nations.

Keynes also began slowly to win the argument that forcing Germany to pay for the war through ruinous reparations would undermine the whole economy of the world. He predicted that a new war would break out within two decades. Twenty years later, in 1939, it did.

The giant fine imposed on Germany was 132 billion marks (about $450 billion in today's money). The Germans actually paid about 20 billion marks by 1931, and more than half came in the form of loans from bankers in New York. But Germany had been the economic powerhouse of Europe before the war, and a major market for British and American goods. If the Germans could no longer afford to buy from Britain and the USA, it would have devastating consequences. The result, warned Keynes, would be economic stagnation. Once again, the arrival of the Great Depression a decade later proved him right.

Ironically, it was Keynes's alliance in the Depression years with his old boss Lloyd George that built the foundations of a new approach, known as Keynesian economics, which proposed more public spending as an approach to tackling the Depression—the very opposite of the Treaty of Versailles. However, Keynes and Lloyd George went their separate ways on how to deal with Hitler's Germany: Lloyd George, appalled by the Treaty of Versailles, which he had negotiated, wanted to appease Hitler; Keynes wanted to rearm and stand up to him.

Recently historians have reappraised the Treaty of Versailles. They have argued that the reparations were never intended to be as severe as they seemed: the vast majority of the huge sum set out was actually a device for fooling audiences back home into believing Germany would pay more than they actually would. The treaty terms were also much more forgiving than the terms Germany planned to impose on the Allies if the roles had been reversed.

That is what happens when nations are fined. If the fines are big enough to work, they tend to undermine the economies of the nations imposing the fines as well. It is the economic version of the old adage that "an eye for an eye makes the whole world blind."

WHAT IF
WE RELIED ON THE PRIVATE SECTOR TO ENFORCE CONTRACTS?

Tim Leunig

 Very few contracts are enforced in law. You would be able to sue if this book contained 50 pages in the middle that read "the quick brown fox jumps over the lazy dog" over and over. But I bet you wouldn't bother. It just wouldn't be worth it. Despite this, no publishers would ever issue a book with filler pages of the kind described because the effect on their reputation would be terrible. "Book publisher cons readers" would be a story on both social and mainstream media. The publishers would be embarrassed and the company would probably go bust. Small traders are more likely to be able to get away with bad service, having no national reputation to worry about. That is why most people choose to deal with builders, say, whom they know, or who have been recommended by friends. So in most cases the law is irrelevant already: local and national reputations are sufficient. The government's ability to enforce contracts only really matters for very big cases. Even that wasn't true in the Middle Ages, so the private sector came up with alternative mechanisms. For example, the Middle Ages saw the creation of "fairs." Merchants wanting to sell their products would pay a small fee to the fair organizers. The organizers checked the merchandise, and required the merchants to use accurate weights and measures. If something went wrong, purchasers could appeal to the organizers. If the organizers agreed with them, the seller would have to make recompense, or be barred from the fair for ever. These rules gave would-be purchasers confidence in trading with people they had never met, and as a result both honest sellers and would-be purchasers flocked to fairs. The government is (usually) more efficient at enforcing contracts, but the private sector can and does step up where necessary.

What Then?

In some countries, particularly the poorest, the rule of law is slow, patchy, or sometimes nonexistent. In these cases people prefer to deal with those they know and trust. People particularly try to avoid dealing with the government, or organizations explicitly or implicitly backed by government. This is because they expect the courts to find for the other side, whatever the merits of the case. Corrupt government can be worse than no government.

What Gives?

370 Average number of days to enforce a contract in the USA.

406 Average number of days to enforce a contract in China.

1,642 Average number of days to enforce a contract in Afghanistan. This is almost four and half years.

What Else?

What if there was no insurance?
See page 140

What if we broke up all the big companies? *See page 144*

WHAT IF WE STOPPED INVENTING THINGS?

Tim Leunig

 People have been inventing things since the world began. Some were small things, like flint knives, while others were immense. The pyramids of ancient Egypt show just how ingenious early peoples could be. Human beings have invented abstract concepts as well as physical things. Concepts such as the rule of law and the number zero are great inventions. Today we appear to have invented absolutely everything we could ever have thought we would need—and some other stuff, as well. And yet still the inventions keep coming, and once we have them we wonder how we did without them. New inventions drive economic progress, so if we stop inventing things, growth will slow, perhaps dramatically. There won't be this year's "must have" flying off the shelves and keeping retailers in business. Those "must have" items also persuade the rest of us to work hard, so that we have the money to buy that exciting new product. Inventions are good for the economy. The end of new things would not stop growth, however, because economic growth also comes from inventing new ways of making existing things. There was nothing particularly special about the Model-T Ford as a car. What was special was the way it was made. Mass production made it cheaper, and that meant that many more people could afford to buy one. Growth would only end if we stopped inventing new things, and stopped inventing new ways to make existing things. Even then, poorer countries would still be able to grow by copying existing global best practice. A world without inventions would also be a very dull world. Imagine if we had created every book, poem, and movie that would ever be made. Imagine if every conceivable picture had already been painted, every photo taken, and every news story already filed. Put like this it is obvious that we will never stop inventing things.

What Then?

There is no limit to our ingenuity. We are inventing cars that can drive themselves, virtually never crash, and go far farther for any given amount of fuel. People are designing glasses that can take photos and videos. Even that most humble of products, laundry detergent, keeps on getting better: clothes can now be washed in less time, using less water, and less energy than ever before. It is hard to imagine a world in which we stop inventing things.

What Gives?

Japan, USA, China, South Korea Top four nations for patent applications in 2010.

20 years Time between marketing of televisions and 100 percent take-up of them in developing countries.

What Else?

What if we stopped buying stuff?
See page 92

What if well-being was the main purpose of economics?
See page 112

WHAT IF
RESOURCES

Bibliography

"Breaking the Mould for Women Leaders: Could Boardroom Quotas Hold the Key?".
Lewis, Rowena and Rake, Katherine. Fawcett Society think piece for the Gender Equality Forum, October 2008.

The Communist Manifesto.
Marx, Karl. 1848.

The Economics of Climate Change.
Stern, Nicholas.
Cambridge University Press, 2007.

The Economic Consequences of the Peace.
Keynes, John Maynard. 1919.

Food and Agriculture Organization of the United Nations. "World Agriculture: Towards 2015/2030 Summary Report." FAO, 2002.

The General Theory of Employment, Interest and Money.
Keynes, John Maynard. 1936.

The Great Crash, 1929.
Galbraith, John Kenneth. 1954.

The Lexus and the Olive Tree: Understanding Globalization.
Friedman, Thomas L.
Farrar, Straus and Giroux, 1999.

"The Rescue that Really Worked."
Guo, J. Newsweek, 22 April 2010.

"So We're Slightly Less Miserable at Work ... Shall We Break Open the Bubbly?".
Ray, Rebecca and Rizzacasa, Thomas. Job Satisfaction: 2012 Edition, June 2012.

A Tract on Monetary Reform.
Keynes, John Maynard. 1923.

Information about global debt:

www.zerohedge.com/article/
total-global-debt-has-double-over-
200-trillion-2020-preserve-
economic-growth

michael-hudson.com/wp-content/
uploads/2010/03/
HudsonLostTradition.pdf

www.economist.com/blogs/
graphicdetail/2012/09/
global-debt-guide

Websites

Association for Heterodox Economics
www.hetecon.net

Economic History Association
eh.net

EconomicsJunkie
www.economicsjunkie.com

Financial Times
www.ft.com

The Incidental Economist
theincidentaleconomist.com

Institute of Economic Affairs
www.iea.org.uk

New Economics Foundation
www.neweconomics.org

New Economics Institute
neweconomicsinstitute.org

Research Papers in Economics
repec.org

Schumacher Center for New Economics
centerforneweconomics.org

Vox
www.voxeu.org

Books

The Case For Working With Your Hands.
Crawford, Matthew.
Penguin Viking, 2010.

Debt: The First 5,000 Years.
Graeber, David.
Melville House Publishing, 2012.

The Economic Naturalist.
Frank, Robert H.
Basic Books, 2008.

*The Great Transformation: The Political
and Economic
Origins of Our Time.*
Polanyi, Karl.
Beacon Press, 2002.

If Women Counted.
Waring, Marilyn.
Harpercollins, 1989.

Keynes: The Return of the Master.
Skidelsky, Robert.
Penguin, 2010.

*Macroeconomics After Keynes:
Reconsideration of the General Theory.*
Chick, Victoria.
MIT Press, 1983.

The New Economics: A Bigger Picture.
Simms, Andrew and Boyle, David.
Routledge, 2009.

The Road to Serfdom.
Hayek, F. A.
Routledge Classics, 2001.

*Small is Beautiful: A Study of Economics
as if People Mattered.*
Schumacher, E. F.
Harper Perennial, 2010.

The Undercover Economist.
Harford, Tim.
Random House, 2007.

*What Then Must We Do? Straight Talk
About the Next American Revolution.*
Alperovitz, Gar.
Chelsea Green Publishing Company, 2013.

*Where Does Money Come From? A Guide
to the UK Monetary & Banking System.*
Ryan-Collins, Josh; Greenham, Tony; Werner,
Richard and Jackson, Andrew.
New Economics Foundation, 2012.

WHAT IF
CONTRIBUTORS

David Boyle is a writer and commentator on economics and history and a former independent reviewer for the UK Cabinet Office and Treasury. His published titles include *Money Matters*, *The Money Changers*, and *Funny Money*. He is a contributor to the *Guardian*, the *New Statesman*, and the *Tablet*.

Tony Greenham is an economist, chartered accountant, and former investment banker who leads research into the financial system at the New Economics Foundation (NEF). He is a regular media commentator and public speaker on money and banking, and is coauthor of many articles, reports, and books on the subject including *Where Does Money Come From? A Guide to the UK Monetary & Banking System*.

Helen Kersley is the head of Valuing What Matters at the New Economics Foundation (NEF). She began her career in the Government Economics Service, specializing in international finance at HM Treasury, and later the European Bank for Reconstruction and Development. Prior to joining NEF, she worked as Research Fellow for four years for Advocacy International, a social enterprise working with low-income country governments, and with organizations working to promote positive development, investment, and environmental sustainability.

Dr. Tim Leunig is an international-prize-winning London School of Economics (LSE) researcher and teacher. As well as writing academic papers, he has written many policy-focused "think tank" reports and has acted as adviser to the UK government and the Organisation for Economic Co-operation and Development (OECD). He has contributed articles to a range of newspapers and magazines, and has appeared extensively on television and radio. He tweets as @timleunig

Ruth Potts is a cofounder of bread, print & roses, a collective engaged in seditious pamphleteering, radical walking, and anarchist baking. She has an MA in Economics for Transition from Schumacher College and was previously Campaign Co-ordinator for the Great Transition at the New Economics Foundation (NEF). She coauthored NEF's Clone Town Britain reports, coordinated media for the Green New Deal Group, organized international conferences on economic transformation, ran a campaign on bank reform, and has organized sell-out events at London's Southbank Centre.

Andrew Simms is the author of several books, including the bestselling *Tescopoly*. He trained at the London School of Economics (LSE) and was described by *New Scientist* magazine as, "a master at joined-up progressive thinking." Andrew is a long-standing campaigner who coined the term "Clone Towns" in work on the fate of the UK's "high streets" and local economic regeneration. He coauthored the ground-breaking Green New Deal, was one of the original organizers of the Jubilee 2000 campaign to cancel poor country debt, cofounded climate campaign onehundredmonth.org, and devised "ecological debt day." After witnessing at first hand over two decades of failed international efforts to solve critical problems ranging from extreme poverty to climate change, his latest book *Cancel the Apocalypse: the New Path to Prosperity* is the result of a search for something better.

WHAT IF
INDEX

WHAT IF
ACKNOWLEDGMENTS

Picture Credits

The publisher would like to thank the following individuals and organizations for their kind permission to reproduce the images in this book. Every effort has been made to acknowledge the pictures, and we apologize if there are any inadvertent omissions.

Image on page 105 is from iStockphoto/Hulton Archive.

All other images are from Shutterstock, Inc. www.shutterstock.com